Understanding
The Merchant of Venice

The Greenwood Press "Literature in Context" Series
Student Casebooks to Issues, Sources, and Historical Documents

The Adventures of Huckleberry Finn
by Claudia Durst Johnson

Animal Farm
by John Rodden

Anne Frank's *The Diary of a Young Girl*
by Hedda Rosner Kopf

The Call of the Wild
by Claudia Durst Johnson

The Catcher in the Rye
by Sanford and Ann Pinsker

The Crucible
by Claudia Durst Johnson
and Vernon E. Johnson

Death of a Salesman
by Brenda Murphy and
Susan C. W. Abbotson

The Grapes of Wrath
by Claudia Durst Johnson

Great Expectations
by George Newlin

The Great Gatsby
by Dalton Gross and
MaryJean Gross

Hamlet
by Richard Corum

I Know Why the Caged Bird Sings
by Joanne Megna-Wallace

Jamaica Kincaid's *Annie John*
by Deborah Mistron

The Literature of World War II
by James H. Meredith

Lord of the Flies
by Kirstin Olsen

Macbeth
by Faith Nostbakken

Of Mice and Men, The Red Pony, and
The Pearl
by Claudia Durst Johnson

Othello
by Faith Nostbakken

Pride and Prejudice
by Debra Teachman

A Raisin in the Sun
by Lynn Domina

The Red Badge of Courage
by Claudia Durst Johnson

Richard Wright's *Black Boy*
by Robert Felgar

Romeo and Juliet
by Alan Hager

The Scarlet Letter
by Claudia Durst Johnson

Shakespeare's *Julius Caesar*
by Thomas Derrick

A Tale of Two Cities
by George Newlin

Things Fall Apart
by Kalu Ogbaa

To Kill a Mockingbird
by Claudia Durst Johnson

Zora Neale Hurston's *Their Eyes
Were Watching God*
by Neal A. Lester

UNDERSTANDING
The Merchant of Venice

A STUDENT CASEBOOK TO ISSUES, SOURCES, AND HISTORICAL DOCUMENTS

Jay L. Halio

The Greenwood Press
"Literature in Context" Series
Claudia Durst Johnson, Series Editor

GREENWOOD PRESS
Westport, Connecticut • London

*New Lenox
Public Library District
120 Veterans Parkway
New Lenox, Illinois 60451*

Library of Congress Cataloging-in-Publication Data

Halio, Jay L.
  Understanding The merchant of Venice : a student casebook to issues, sources, and historical documents / Jay L. Halio.
    p.   cm.—(The Greenwood Press "Literature in context" series, ISSN 1074–598X)
    Includes bibliographical references (p.   ) and index.
    ISBN 0–313–31011–4 (alk. paper)
    1. Shakespeare, William, 1564–1616. Merchant of Venice.   2. Shakespeare, William, 1564–1616. Merchant of Venice—Sources.   3. Shylock (Fictitious character)   4. Jews in literature.   5. Comedy.   I. Title.   II. Series.
  PR2825.H35   2000
  822.3'3—dc21   99–462053

British Library Cataloguing in Publication Data is available.

Library of Congress Catalog Card Number: 99–462053
ISBN: 0–313–31011–4
ISSN: 1074–598X

First published in 2000

Greenwood Press, 88 Post Road West, Westport, CT 06881
An imprint of Greenwood Publishing Group, Inc.
www.greenwood.com

Printed in the United States of America

The paper used in this book complies with the
Permanent Paper Standard issued by the National
Information Standards Organization (Z39.48–1984).

10 9 8 7 6 5 4 3 2 1

For Rae Russo

Contents

Contents

Preface

When Barbara Rader first invited me to do this casebook on *The Merchant of Venice*, I was not sure I could or should accept her kind invitation. Although I had written and edited many books, including conventional casebooks—collections of essays by modern critics—I had never done the kind of book she proposed, especially one for high school students and teachers. But the more I thought about it, the more I found the invitation appealing. High schools, after all, are where many more students study and learn than in colleges and universities, where I have spent all of my professional life. It seemed like an opportunity to make a real difference in the way students and their teachers approach Shakespeare's most controversial play.

Although I had done a scholarly edition of *The Merchant of Venice* in 1993, I found—as scholars inevitably do when they restudy one of Shakespeare's plays—that there was still a good deal more to learn. I am grateful to the Folger Shakespeare Library in Washington, DC, where most of the basic research was carried on, for once again affording me the use of their excellent resources and for the many kindnesses of their incomparable staff. I am grateful, too, to the University of Delaware for granting me a leave of absence to continue my research. Debts are also owed to Lynn Malloy, who succeeded Barbara Rader as managing editor for this series at Greenwood Press, and to the general editor, Claudia Durst Johnson, for their many useful suggestions—and for their patience and understanding as I grappled with the, to me, new and sometimes baffling ways of approaching a work designed primarily for high school students and their teachers. I owe thanks also to that excellent high school teacher, Tom Lederer, for lending me many useful materials; to Georgiana Ziegler for checking several references for me while I was in residence at the University of Cyprus; and to Liz Leiba, who worked so diligently as copyeditor. Rebecca Ardwin, senior production editor, and Leanne Small, assistant manager, editorial administration, were most helpful in seeing this volume into print. To them I am very grateful as well. Any errors or oversights that persist are entirely my responsibility.

Finally, I dedicate this book to my aunt, Rae Russo, the last of my father's and mother's generation, whose pride in my achievements serves to inspire further efforts to become worthy of her feelings for me and my work.

Introduction

The Merchant of Venice is Shakespeare's most controversial play. Its alleged anti-Semitism continues to engage both literary critics and theatrical reviewers every time the play is staged or a new edition is published. Although Shylock appears in only five scenes, he dominates the action. Nonetheless, the casket scenes are also important and provide much of the play's color and suspense. In fact, the play raises many important issues today, perhaps even more than in the 1590s, when it was first produced and printed.

Among the many issues that merit discussion, besides the central one of anti-Semitism, are the relationships between parents and children (there are three sets of them in the play), particularly involving permission to marry, the position of women in society generally, justice and mercy, friendship, matrimony, and the various kinds of bonds that connect human beings with each other. Another important issue, one raised by the very existence of a moneylender, Shylock, in the play, is the problem of usury. Christian doctrine generally opposed lending money at interest and exerted tremendous political pressure to prohibit it in England during the sixteenth century. Venice, as a center of world trade during this period and a place where many tourists flocked, then as now, was an exotic and intriguing locale—as were other cities in Europe— that attracted the interest of playwrights and their audiences. These focuses of concern and others, such as performing the play in the contemporary theater, will be treated in the ensuing chapters.

To present a historical context for *The Merchant of Venice* and its issues, a selection of excerpts from historical documents provides the substance of the material contained in this book. Elizabethans read and traveled a good deal and wrote about their travels. What they saw and how they reacted, especially to Venice and its people, may be typified in the accounts of two inveterate travelers, Thomas Coryat and Fynes Moryson, extracts from whose writings make interesting, vivid, and perceptive reading. How their accounts of Venice and Italy compare with Shakespeare's recreation of those places in *The Merchant of Venice* is very worthwhile exploring. Whether Shakespeare himself ever visited Italy, we do not know, but two of his plays, *Othello* as well as *The Merchant of Venice*, are set largely in Venice, and several of his other plays, such as *Romeo and Juliet* and *Two Gentlemen of Verona*, are set elsewhere in sixteenth-century Italy. Far-off Italy and her cities were literally wonderful places for Elizabethans to imagine, contemplate, or, like Coryat and Moryson, to visit. For many Britons and Americans today they still are; for no matter how much Venice and other Italian cities have changed, they still retain a good deal of the splendor and mystery that were admired in the Renaissance.

The position of women today is far different from what it was in Shakespeare's time, and to understand the differences we need to know more about how women were regarded. Since marriage, including elopement, is a major focus in *The Merchant of Venice*, we also need to learn what Shakespeare's contemporaries thought about it, how they arranged it, and what role parents played (or wanted to play). In addition, we can learn about what qualities in potential husbands and wives were stressed in the various handbooks on marriage that were published. A great deal was written about this important enterprise, because for a very long time, right up until World War II, marriage was permanently binding; at least, a divorce or annulment was extremely difficult if not impossible to obtain, unlike today. Men and women, therefore, were advised to take matrimony very seriously, which is one reason that Portia's father in *The Merchant of Venice* wrote his will the way he did and established the choice of caskets—containers, or chests, containing objects and scrolls—as a means of finding the best suitor for his daughter. Intermarriage between people of different faiths was another problem that concerned clergymen as well as parents, and in the Jessica-Lorenzo subplot in *The Merchant of Venice* it becomes an issue.

Relationships between men and women and parents and children were not the only important ones in Shakespeare's age. Taking their cue from classical treatises on the subject, some believed that friendships between men were of a higher order and thus more important. The great Roman orator and essayist Cicero, or Tully as he was known, was justly famous at a time when most education was conducted through Latin texts. He was famous not only for his style, but for the substance of his writing, as in his long treatise on friendship, excerpted here. Sir Thomas Elyot, one of the early Tudor humanists in the court of Henry VIII, greatly admired Cicero and adopted many of his views in his very influential book called *The Governor*. Many friendships appear in *The Merchant of Venice*, chiefly that between Antonio and Bassanio, which must have suggested to Elizabethans in Shakespeare's audience the biblical friendship of David and Jonathan or the classical friendship of Damon and Pythias. Other similar friendships were recorded and publicized wherein a man was willing to lay down his life for his friend, as in these examples, and as Antonio is prepared to do for Bassanio. Whether any of these friendships or the ones in *The Merchant of Venice* involved latent or overt homosexuality is another issue we may wish to consider.

For a proper understanding of Shakespeare's play, we need to know something, too, about the way Jews were regarded in the Renaissance and throughout English and European history. Fortunately, a wealth of material has been unearthed on this subject, an important part having to do with events in London when Shakespeare was writing or thinking about writing *The Merchant of Venice*. In 1594, for example, a Jew, Dr. Roderigo Lopez, was tried and convicted of trying to poison Queen Elizabeth, and at this time Marlowe's play, *The Jew of Malta* (1588), was revived. So was a striking contrast to that play, *An Enterlude of the Vertuous and Godly Queene Hester*, which dramatizes the story of Queen Esther, Ahasuerus, and Haman—the story of Purim—celebrated among Jews to this day but also well known among Shakespeare's Christian audience. The attitude of the church toward Jews was also extremely important and influential, and it was by no means simple. Both Catholics and Protestants wrote voluminously on the subject, and it is useful to know what Luther, Calvin, and others thought as England became a Protestant country after the sixteenth-century Reformation.

The whole problem of usury, or moneylending for profit, also occupied both religious and secular leaders to the point where several different laws were passed in England under its Tudor monarchs to prohibit or to regulate the practice as it was known during this period. Debates raged in Parliament until a compromise bill was passed in 1571 called the Act against Usury, which stated that usury was morally wrong but nevertheless permitted lending at interest at a rate not to exceed 10 percent. As in the controversy over the attitude toward Jews, Catholics and Protestants differed between and among themselves over the matter of usury, some finding it utterly deplorable and reprehensible, others recognizing the practical need for some form of moneylending at interest provided that it was not injurious to anyone or excessive. Jews, who were not the only ones involved in moneylending, also pondered the problems involved in lending to others outside of their religion. The focus for much of this discussion was the interpretation of some verses in Scripture and the translation of key words from the Hebrew in the Old Testament. In *The Merchant of Venice* lending at interest is a major conflict between Antonio, who eschews the practice, and Shylock, who profits from it.

Finally, we need to ask how these many issues are relevant today. Chapter 7 explores contemporary applications and concludes with a section on the way the play has been and is being performed on the modern stage. As in the preceding chapters, excerpts from appropriate publications, including the editorial pages of leading American newspapers, will help focus on these contemporary applications. But before attempting to understand *The Merchant of Venice* in either its historical or contemporary context, we need to know what happens in the play, how it is structured, what themes are developed, and what techniques Shakespeare uses. That is the purpose of Chapter 1 of this book, which begins with a consideration of the play's genre. How Shakespeare used the sources from which he borrowed is also important in helping us understand what he was doing, especially in the ways he altered or added to his sources. Like his contemporaries, Shakespeare was not constrained to invent his plots. His audiences were more interested in the way he dramatized familiar legends and tales, and what new

perceptions as well as entertainments he could provide by so doing. The audiences also delighted in multiple plots and subplots,
the use of blank verse and songs, fresh imagery, and other poetic
devices Shakespeare and his fellow dramatists used, which may
appear unfamiliar to us today but are not wholly inaccessible if we
attend carefully to them and recognize how they operate.

Because of the timeliness—or timelessness—of the issues Shakespeare treats, *The Merchant of Venice* has held the interest of audiences and readers for centuries. Like *Hamlet*, it is full of
intriguing inconsistencies and contradictions, and that may be another source of its fascination. It is not that Shakespeare did not
know what he was doing. A consummate playwright approaching
the apex of his career when he wrote *The Merchant of Venice*, he
well understood the complexity of life, of human nature, and his
vision had begun to become characterized by what a modern critic,
Norman Rabkin, has called "complementarity," that is, the ability
to see many sides of an issue or problem. That is why a simplistic
approach to his plays is invariably fruitless and needs to be replaced by what another scholar, Rosalie Colie, in writing about
King Lear, has called "prismatic" criticism. For Shakespeare's plays
lend themselves, whether in Renaissance or modern dress, to a
wide variety of interpretations, many of which demand serious
consideration. To help us understand *The Merchant of Venice* and
the many themes and issues it contains, both in its historical context and in its importance for us today, is the purpose of this book.

As an aid to accomplishing this purpose, at the end of each chapter or section a list of topics for discussion and further study will
be found. Some will direct students to the excerpts included in
that section; others will require further reading or connecting the
excerpts with the play under study. Still others may raise contemporary issues that confront us in our daily lives.

Since students have many different interests, this casebook aims
to help develop those interests in a multicultural framework. No
one approach to *The Merchant of Venice* will satisfy everyone's
interest, but a combined or multifaceted approach may bring not
only fuller understanding but also greater fulfillment. No literature
exists in an intellectual, social, or political vacuum, any more than
individuals alive today do or did at other times. By utilizing more
than one approach to understanding *The Merchant of Venice*, we
will experience the play more completely. At the same time,

we will see how the different approaches truly complement each other. This is part of the not-so-hidden agenda of this book.

All quotations from *The Merchant of Venice* are from the version of the play edited by Jay L. Halio and published by Oxford University Press (1993). Quotations from other plays are from the *Complete Works of William Shakespeare*, edited by Stanley Wells and Gary Taylor et al., also published by Oxford (1988). Quotations from Renaissance texts have been rendered into modern American spelling and punctuation.

1

Literary and Dramatic Analysis

The first question that *The Merchant of Venice* raises is, What kind of play is this? Is it a comedy, tragedy, tragi-comedy (a play that starts tragically but ends like a comedy), or what? Written in the mid-1590s, when Shakespeare's art was rapidly maturing, it shows the playwright experimenting with a variety of forms. He had just written the three plays of his "lyric period": a comedy, *A Midsummer Night's Dream*; a romantic tragedy, *Romeo and Juliet*; and a history play chronicling the rise and fall of King Richard II. Some aspects of *The Merchant of Venice* derive from all three of these plays: its beautiful lyric poetry, found, for example, in Lorenzo's monologues in act 5; the comic antics of the clown, Lancelot Gobbo; and the downfall of Shylock. For modern audiences, however, the play raises certain issues that have led some critics to regard this play as a "problem play"; that is, a drama that raises significant moral questions that it fails satisfactorily to resolve, as in Shylock's forced conversion at the end of act 4, scene 1.

Shakespeare wrote *The Merchant of Venice* at a time when few Jews lived in England, from where they had been forcibly expelled in 1290 by Edward I. Nevertheless, the Jew remained a powerful image in English literature and drama throughout the succeeding ages (see Chapter 3). The trial and execution of Queen Elizabeth's physician, Dr. Roderigo Lopez, in 1594; the revival of Marlowe's play, *The Jew of Malta*; and other events aroused renewed anti-Semitism in England and may have led Shakespeare to contemplate writing about a rich Jewish moneylender who, like Barabas in Marlowe's play, acts the role of a villain. But unlike Marlowe, Shakespeare endowed his villain Shylock with some very human qualities that evoke much sympathy. The result is an ambivalence toward Shylock that makes his role one of the most dramatically complex and compelling among all of Shakespeare's characters, and one that reinforces the sense of this work as a problem play.

Shylock, of course, is not the only important character in *The Merchant of Venice*, which takes its title from Antonio, the Venetian merchant who borrows from Shylock to help his friend, Bassanio. Portia, the rich heiress whom Bassanio courts, is another major character, and the relationship between her and her suitors also raises important moral issues. Is Bassanio mainly after Portia's money, or is there a genuine love between the two? How does Bassanio's friendship with Antonio complicate his relationship with Portia? These are questions that the play raises and tries to resolve. To what extent they are resolved more or less successfully is something that literary and dramatic analysis must consider, as we shall do in the pages that follow.

SHAKESPEARE'S USE OF HIS SOURCES

Like his contemporaries, Shakespeare borrowed freely from previously known works for his plots, characters, and themes. He also invented new twists and turns in his narrative as well as new characters to give his plays fresh appeal, often providing a new perspective on events. Writers have always done this, avoiding charges of plagiarism by their inventiveness. For Elizabethans, the important thing was not the originality of the story, but the imaginativeness of its presentation—the way it was developed, the language used to tell it, and the new slant that emerged from the tale. Shakespeare could, if he wished, invent his own plots, as he did for *A Midsummer Night's Dream* and *The Tempest*, but for most of his plays he seemed more interested in reusing old or familiar stories and themes to see what he could do with them. By comparing Shakespeare's play with his sources, then, we can glimpse something of his creative processes at work, noting how he altered certain details and added or omitted others, and then asking what the results of the differences are.

Shakespeare's main source for *The Merchant of Venice* was a sixteenth-century Italian novel, *Il Pecorone* (*The Dunce*) by Ser Giovanni Fiorentino. In this story, Ansaldo, godfather to Gianetto, finances the young man's attempts to win the Lady of Belmonte, a rich widow who requires her suitors to consummate their love before she agrees to wed them, or lose everything they have brought with them. Twice Gianetto fails the test, because of a drink that has been drugged, until the third time, when one of the lady's waiting-women, taking pity on the young man, warns him not to drink. Meanwhile, to subsidize this third voyage, Ansaldo has had to borrow funds from a Jewish moneylender and forfeit a pound of his flesh if the debt is not repaid on time. Enjoying his good fortune, Gianetto forgets all about the loan until it is too late, but then hurries back to Venice with more than enough money from his wife to repay the debt and save his godfather. The lady, in disguise as a lawyer, follows close behind. When the Jew refuses ten times the amount of the debt and insists on having his pound of flesh, the lady saves the day by requiring the Jew to take exactly one pound without a single drop of blood. Frustrated, the Jew tears up the bond and leaves without so much as the principal allowed to him. The young couple then return to Belmonte, where Ansaldo weds the waiting-woman who had aided Gianetto.

One immediately notices certain differences between Shakespeare's play and his main source. For example, while the moneylender is foiled in his plan to kill Antonio, he is not forced to convert to Christianity at the end; he is only deprived of the money he has lent. Another important difference is the test that Gianetto undergoes as compared with the three caskets in *The Merchant of Venice* from which Portia's suitors must choose. For this part of the plot, Shakespeare had recourse to a story in the *Gesta Romanorum*, where a young woman must choose the right casket before the king will approve the marriage to his son. Perhaps Shakespeare preferred to complicate the plot, introduce more characters, and suggest a significant moral element by having Portia's suitors tested with a choice of caskets. Through the casket plot the characters of Portia and Bassanio are also more fully developed than their counterparts in *Il Pecorone*. But the ring plot, through which Portia tests the loyalty of Bassanio at the end of the trial scene, derives from *Il Pecorone* and is used in the same way. Still disguised as a lawyer, Portia gets Bassanio to give her the ring she had given him earlier and he had promised never to relinquish.

Another difference that Shakespeare introduced involves the subplot of Lorenzo and Jessica. Here he probably drew on Marlowe's play, where Barabas's daughter, Abigail, falls in love with a Christian and wishes to marry him. Barabas foils their hopes, first by having Abigail's lover killed and then by killing his daughter, who has converted to Christianity and entered a nunnery. Shakespeare did not follow these unfortunate details but turned instead to another Italian novel, Masuccio's fifteenth-century *Il Novellino*, story 14, in which an old miser has a lovely young daughter whom he carefully sequesters at home. Nevertheless, she successfully elopes with a clever young nobleman, despite all the precautions her father has taken. After the couple are happily married and the bride becomes pregnant, a feast is held to which the old father is invited and becomes reconciled with his daughter and her husband. In this story, unlike Shakespeare's adaptation of it, no question of an interfaith marriage is raised.

Shakespeare resorted to some other sources for several details in his drama, but these are the main ones. Even from this very brief summary we can see how he reshaped them to fashion what is essentially a new and more complex rendering. The whole issue of conversion to Christianity is a new element in Shakespeare's representation, but equally important though in a different way are the dramatic construction, the characterizations, and the poetry of *The Merchant of Venice*, to which we must now turn.

POETIC AND DRAMATIC PATTERNS

Despite its controversial or problematic nature, *The Merchant of Venice* contains some of the most lyrical and lovely passages in all of Shakespeare. Many of these passages, like Portia's famous lines on the quality of mercy (4.1.181–99) or Lorenzo's on music and the beauty of the night (5.1.54–65), are worth committing to memory. These set speeches, as they are sometimes called, like the arias in a Verdi opera, delight audiences even as they help develop the dramatic action. But Shakespeare's prose is also important, and we sometimes forget that he was not only a consummate poet but an excellent prose writer as well. Shylock's defense of himself at 3.1.50–69 is one of the most spirited and vigorous pieces of prose ever constructed. Taken out of context, it is often used as a vindication of Shylock's humanity, but in context it works not only as that but as a criticism of Christian behavior. Like Portia on mercy, this is one of the most memorable speeches in the play.

Although Shakespeare at first followed his predecessors among Tudor dramatists in using a great deal of rhymed couplets, by the time he wrote *The Merchant of Venice* blank verse had become the mainstay of poetic drama. It continued to be used throughout Elizabethan drama and during the reign of James I, gaining in strength and virtuosity while it ever more closely resembled the spoken language of men and women.

Blank Verse

Blank verse basically consists of ten-syllable, unrhymed lines with alternating stresses on the second, fourth, sixth, eighth, and tenth syllables. The stresses may vary—sometimes a good deal— for a number of reasons. For example, when the author wishes to bring emphasis to a word that might not otherwise be accented, or when he simply wishes to avoid falling into too regular a pattern of stressed and unstressed syllables, which can become monotonous. Occasionally, to signal the end of a scene as at 1.1.184–85, or a stretch of sententiae (proverbial wisdom), Shakespeare used rhymed couplets, often varying the meter at the same time, as at 2.7.65–73.

Songs also are important in Shakespeare's plays. *The Merchant of Venice* contains only one song, but it is a very important one. It appears in 3.2 as Bassanio approaches the caskets to make his choice. Critics have commented on how the first three lines all rhyme with "lead." They argue that this song seems to be a clue Portia gives Bassanio, directing him how to choose the right one, especially since no such song appears in the other casket scenes with the Prince of Morocco or the Prince of Aragon. Be that as it may—Bassanio does not seem to hear the song, and Portia's integrity would be seriously damaged if it is true—the song provides a pleasant interlude and preparation for the theme of Bassanio's speech, "So may the outward shows be least themselves" (3.2.73 ff.).

Image and Metaphor

As we might expect in a play about merchants, much of the language derives from commercial transactions, even when it may appear rather inappropriate, as when Portia addresses Bassanio after he has chosen the leaden casket:

> You see me, Lord Bassanio, where I stand,
> Such as I am. Though for myself alone
> I would not be ambitious in my wish
> To wish myself much better, yet for you
> I would be trebled twenty times myself,
> A thousand times more fair, ten thousand times more rich,
> That only to stand high in your account
> I might in virtues, beauties, livings, friends
> Exceed account. But the full sum of me
> Is sum of something which, to term in gross,
> Is an unlessoned girl. . . . (3.2.149–59)

Nerissa and Graziano's phrasing in the speeches that follow soon after, when they announce their wish to be married too, re-emphasize the commercial aspect of the transaction. Nerissa comments that they have seen their wishes "prosper" (3.2.187), and Graziano speaks of the "bargain" of the faith that Portia and Bassanio have pledged to each other (3.2.193). Near the end of this part of the dialogue, when Graziano proposes a bet, "We'll play with them the first boy for a thousand ducats" (3.2.213), money once again becomes a pronounced consideration.

Since Shakespeare was writing for a largely literate audience and not merely for the masses that also populated his theater, he felt free also to use many classical allusions. Graziano combines both kinds of language when he greets Lorenzo and Jessica at 3.2.239: "We are the Jasons, we have won the fleece." Here he compares Bassanio and himself to the ancient argonaut Jason on his dangerous voyage to Colchis on the Black Sea in quest of the golden fleece, one of the most famous prizes in classical literature. The speeches of the Prince of Morocco in 2.1 are studded with classical allusions, although he gets some of them wrong, an indication of the way Shakespeare makes fun of his pretentiousness. For example, the prince confuses the story of Hercules and Lichas playing at dice with another story of Hercules thrown into a rage by the shirt of Nessus. Shakespeare's audience would have picked up the allusions and understood how Morocco mixed them up.

Shakespeare's audience was also steeped in biblical lore. With the advent of the Bishops' Bible and the Geneva Bible and other English translations made available under Elizabeth I's Protestant rule, more and more English people read Scripture on their own, besides hearing it read to them in church every Sunday. Shakespeare could count on his audience therefore to grasp the allusions made directly, as in Shylock's account of Jacob and Laban in 1.3, or indirectly, as at 3.1.80–81 where Shylock alludes to the curse upon his people mentioned in Matthew 27.25 and Luke 13.34–35. Like metaphors, these allusions extend the frame of reference and thus help provide a broader context for the play than might at first seem apparent.

Although no single strand of imagery pervades *The Merchant of Venice* in the way that imagery of blood pervades *Macbeth* or imagery of disease pervades *Hamlet*, the frequent suggestion of music contributes significantly to the play's atmosphere, according to Caroline Spurgeon, who pioneered the study of image patterns in Shakespeare's plays. The two great moments of emotion and romance—Bassanio's casket scene and especially Lorenzo and Jessica's evening scene in 5.1—are dominated by music. Lorenzo summons musicians to play while he and his wife await Portia's return, commenting, "Soft stillness and the night / Become the touches of sweet harmony" (56–57). He is then moved to remark on the music of the spheres, the heavenly harmony that exists in "immortal souls" (60–65). But as the music begins to play, Jessica says she is never merry when she hears sweet music. She means that music puts her into a mood of contemplation, and in a long speech Lorenzo explains the reason for that, alluding to the poet Orpheus in Ovid's *Metamorphoses*. The point of those passages, in part, is to restore the play to the realm of romantic comedy, disturbed as it was by the events of the trial scene in the immediately preceding act. It also looks forward to what happens at the end of the scene: the reunions and reconciliations of the other two married couples and the good news that Portia delivers to Antonio, Lorenzo, and Jessica. As elsewhere in Shakespeare, music is the symbol of harmony. By contrast, in act 2, where a good deal of music and revelry is suggested, Shylock declares his antipathy to masques and music (2.5.28–36), one of many contrasts the play develops between Shylock and his antagonists.

Many poetical images appear throughout *The Merchant of Venice* consistent with the lyrical spirit that pervades much of the play. Salarino's pageant of argosies at 1.1.9–14 is one such example. Using an elaborate simile, he compares Antonio's state of mind to his sailing ships tossing on the ocean, an image he continues in his next speech. Jessica's comments on her embarrassed disguise as a boy as she prepares to elope with Lorenzo is delightfully witty, as she comments on the nature of love, invoking the image of blind Cupid, the little love god:

> I am glad 'tis night, you do not look on me,
> For I am much ashamed of my exchange.
> But love is blind, and lovers cannot see
> The pretty follies they themselves commit;
> For if they could, Cupid himself would blush
> To see me thus transformed to a boy. (2.6.34–39)

Antonio's description of himself as a "tainted wether of the flock" (4.1.113–15) is a rather different example. It shows how Antonio interprets his state of mind in the final scene before Portia enters; he then uses another image to reveal further the depth of his despondency.

Stage Conventions

Like his fellow dramatists, Shakespeare used a number of stage conventions, or artificial dramatic devices, to develop his plots. Perhaps the most difficult Elizabethan stage convention for modern audiences to grasp is what is called impenetrable disguise. When Portia appears as Dr. Balthazar in 4.1, neither her husband, Bassanio, nor anyone else recognizes her or Nerissa, disguised as her clerk. On stage their costumes, makeup, and voice intonations all help conceal their true identities, but even so, the audience, who have been apprised beforehand, easily recognizes who they are, though their husbands cannot. In *A Midsummer Night's Dream* when Oberon says he is invisible but remains in plain view of the audience, he is invisible to the characters on stage. This requires the same imaginative acceptance as other stage conventions, such as the aside and the soliloquy. When a character speaks an aside, for example, only the audience hears him or her, notwithstanding that the speech is perfectly audible to everyone on stage. An example of such an aside is Shylock's speech as Antonio enters at 1.3.38–49. Lancelot Gobbo's monologue that opens 2.2 is an example of a soliloquy, a speech spoken to the audience that, like Hamlet's famous soliloquies, allows us to hear what a character is thinking and is similar to the voice-over technique used today in films and television dramas.

All conventions, like the overall illusion that dramatic representation involves, depend on an audience's acceptance of what Samuel Taylor Coleridge called a "willing suspension of disbelief." While a good deal of Shakespearean drama is realistic, not all of it is: ghosts appear, as in *Julius Caesar* and *Macbeth*, and gods descend from the heavens, as in *As You Like It* and *Cymbeline*. At the end of *The Merchant of Venice* at least one unexplained miracle occurs, when Portia announces that three of Antonio's argosies have safely come to harbor, and Lorenzo alludes to another when he says that Portia drops manna in the way of starved people (5.1.294–95). The reality that Shakespeare appeals to more than any other is the reality of the imagination, which is more powerful than any other kind of reality.

Characterization

Discussion of reality prompts a discussion of the nature of dramatic character. To what extent are the characters in Shakespeare's plays, and specifically those in *The Merchant of Venice*, "real" people? Some critics argue that dramatic characters, like characters in a novel, are not real but convey only the illusion of people in real life. They lack any existence before the play begins as well as after it ends. As Prospero says in *The Tempest*, their "little lives are rounded with a sleep." The illusion, however, is sometimes so powerful that we cannot help thinking of dramatic characters as actual historical personages. While few people today would go so far as to describe the girlhood of Shakespeare's heroines, as one nineteenth-century critic, Mary Cowden Clarke, did in a book bearing that title, many modern critics do not hesitate to explore the psychological motivations that underlie a character's actions. Character motivation of course is important in any play or novel; without sufficient motivation a character's behavior will lack credibility. This is where illusion and reality meet.

A discussion of *The Merchant of Venice*, therefore, inevitably involves character analysis, just as all of Shakespeare's plays do. Some analysis will continue to baffle us as it has done others. What, for instance, is the cause of Antonio's melancholy, announced in the play's opening line? Solanio and Salarino offer some explanations, but Antonio rejects all of them. We never do find out the reason, and Antonio himself remains baffled. At the end he seems relieved to know that his ships have all come in safely to harbor, but does that end his melancholy? And what caused it in the first place? Since the play does not provide the answers to these questions, we can only speculate on the reasons.

Bassanio's motivation in seeking out Portia is by no means simple, either. While he undoubtedly finds her attractive, as she does him, is love the main motivation for Bassanio's quest? Or does her wealth also have a lot to do with it? Can the two motives be separated, or are they inextricably intertwined? Probably the latter, as is the case with some other couples in Shakespeare's plays. (Shakespeare may be a romantic, but he is not a sentimentalist.) And what occasions Jessica's long silence at the end of the play? Her last words are, "I am never merry when I hear sweet music" (5.1.69). Lorenzo then reads her a lecture on the power of music to alter states of being in people as in animals. While his explanation may be convincing, is it altogether so? Or is something else bothering Jessica? In many recent productions, directors make a good deal of her apparent brooding on events (see Chapter 7), although in a comedy it is expected that she should be as joyous as the other couples who enter Portia's house.

Finally, what motivates Shylock to accept conversion to Christianity as a means of saving his life? For a Jew, the one biblical command that may not be broken is the command not to take any other God before Jehovah. Shylock clearly violates this command, as he has violated other commands in his faith. Have the Christians broken his spirit to such an extent that he no longer has any integrity left whatsoever? Or is he merely a craven moneylender after all? His behavior has sometimes been interpreted either way, for in this respect the play remains tantalizingly ambiguous. Again, is Antonio's mercy really that, or is it a more sinister kind of revenge than even Shylock's demand for his pound of flesh was? Some critics favor the first explanation, arguing that Shakespeare's audience believed salvation could come only through Christianity. But others, especially in our post-Holocaust days, find the demand for Shylock's conversion not unlike the cruelty of the Spanish inquisition.

Multiple Plots and Subplots

Shakespeare borrowed not from one but several sources for *The Merchant of Venice*, fusing the casket plot, taken from the *Gesta Romanorum*, to the quest plot in Ser Giovanni's *Il Pecorone*. He did this not only to vary his narrative, but also to contrast different types of characters with the different types of caskets. Morocco, Aragon, and Bassanio all differ from each other, as they differ from the first group of suitors mentioned in act 1, scene 2. Shakespeare also inserted the subplot of Jessica and Lorenzo's elopement to show yet another kind of romantic courtship. At the same time, this subplot brings out aspects of Shylock's character that may make him more or less sympathetic. Much depends on how it is interpreted and portrayed, particularly on how we see Shylock's relationship with his daughter. She claims "Our house is hell" (2.3.2), but Jessica may simply be a discontented young woman bridling at her father's austerity. Shylock, however, may not be the kind of loving parent she wants and needs, a factor motivating her rebelliousness.

Juxtaposition in Elizabethan Drama

One of the basic techniques of Elizabethan drama, which was performed without intermission from start to finish (act intervals came later in the seventeenth century), was the juxtaposition of scenes, one against the other. In this way the action of the scenes could be seen to comment upon each other. For example, Antonio's melancholy opens the play and is followed in the next scene by Portia's world-weariness. Shakespeare evidently intends a comparison or contrast between the two important characters and expects us to notice how their problems are ultimately resolved—if they are.

Sometimes the juxtapositions occur within a scene. In act 3, scene 1, Solanio and Salarino begin by discussing Antonio's disasters at sea and then turn to Shylock's misfortunes as the latter enters. What does Antonio's ill luck have to do with Shylock's lament for the loss of his daughter? What makes Salarino, after taunting Shylock rather unmercifully, bring up Antonio's losses at sea? Are they merely idle gossipers, or do they have some sinister motive? The play offers no answer to this question, but note that it is precisely here that Shylock first says that he may foreclose on his bond with Antonio. Only a deeply disturbed individual could see in that action anything like an appropriate revenge for Jessica's elopement with Lorenzo. It smacks of the worst kind of spitefulness, however justified it might otherwise appear. Later on, in the trial scene Portia will juxtapose the advantages of mercy as opposed to justice and instruct all those present as well as Shylock on the quality of mercy. She delays resolving the difficulty Antonio is in until almost the last moment not only to heighten the suspense of the scene and intensify the dramatic events that follow, but also to give Shylock every opportunity to relent.

Finally, Shakespeare retains the ring plot from *Il Pecorone* for his last two scenes, compounding it by having Nerissa also get her ring back from Graziano. Through the ring plot these wives teach their husbands a good lesson about marital loyalty, which in their view supersedes the loyalty between friends. For this reason, Portia gives the ring to Antonio to return to Bassanio, thereby symbolically indicating her supremacy over her male rival regarding Bassanio's devotion.

Thematic Development

Several themes have already been suggested in the foregoing analyses of language and character, such as the relation of mercy and justice, the nature of love, and the bonds that connect or tie one human being to another. Themes are the underlying ideas that help to unify the action of a play and develop its meaning. They can be identified in various ways by focusing on key words or images and their repetition throughout the play. Recurrent or contrasting actions by the characters may also suggest themes, just as analysis of the relationship between main plot and subplot often does. Sometimes what seems to be merely a comic interlude may suggest a major theme, just as Lancelot Gobbo's scene with his father suggests the relationship between parent and child that is very much at the heart of *The Merchant of Venice*. Similarly, the dramatic structure of a play may suggest its organizing principle and thereby one of its major themes. For a play need not be limited to a single theme, but on the contrary may have several important themes worthy of analysis.

The major theme in *The Merchant of Venice* is the theme of bondage and bonding. The play deals with all kinds of ties: between father and child, between friend and friend, between master and servant, between creditor and debtor, and so forth. But perhaps the most important bond of all is the one that connects one human being with another, implicit in most of the other types of ties found in this play. The first line of the play also suggests another kind of bond—the way Antonio seems tied to melancholy, a melancholy he is at pains to understand but is unable to. His friends, Salarino and Solanio, try to help him sort out his feelings, but to no avail. Then other friends, Bassanio, Graziano, and Lorenzo, appear. It is not entirely clear what the relationships are between them and the other two friends, who leave the scene rather abruptly, but Antonio reassures Salarino and Solanio that, whatever coolness may have grown between the two groups, these two men are very dear to him. A comic interlude follows during which Graziano tries to cheer up Antonio, as Salarino and Solanio had tried earlier. His jocularity notwithstanding, Graziano delivers some acute observations, such as the way men occasionally try to secure a reputation for wisdom by appearing grave and silent. He then leaves with Lorenzo so that Bassanio may talk privately with Antonio.

The rest of the scene shows the strong bond that ties these two friends together. They are more than just friends; they are almost like father and son, reflecting the relationship between Gianetto and Ansaldo in Shakespeare's source, *Il Pecorone*. But the relationship here is at a later stage, for Bassanio is already in debt to Antonio and is uneasy about once more asking his friend for funds, especially since they will be used to woo a lady for his wife. The potential conflict between friends and lovers (soon to become spouses) is thus introduced, but throughout the play Antonio tries to act as generously as he can. He is even willing, when it comes down to it, to pledge his life so that Bassanio can have sufficient funds to make a good impression when he goes to Belmont to see Portia.

The next scene focuses on another kind of bond, the one that ties a daughter to her father's will. Although Portia at first bridles at this obligation (1.2.21–25), under Nerissa's tutelage she recognizes the virtue inherent in her father's requirement that whoever marries her must first choose the right casket. As Nerissa says, Portia's father was "ever virtuous," and at his death he was inspired to good purpose, sensing that whoever chooses the right casket will be the one Portia will "rightly love" (1.2.27–32). Later in the play, the bond between parent and child is developed in other ways: comically in the scene between Lancelot Gobbo and his father (2.2), and more seriously in the relationship between Shylock and Jessica, who not only deserts her father, but also her religion—another bond that is not as easily broken as Jessica may think.

The third scene introduces several different but related kinds of bonds. The first is the commercial bond, the agreement between creditor and borrower for a certain sum of money. But the bond that ties enemies to each other is also present as well as the attempt to overcome a historic enmity and enter a new relationship. Shylock's attitudes are very peculiar. The contradictions and inconsistencies in his speeches are only part of his strange behavior. On the one hand, he says he hates Antonio and resents his behavior toward him (1.3.38–49, 103–25); on the other hand, he would be friends with Antonio and have his love (1.3.133–38). To this end he is willing to offer a loan *at no interest*. For a moneylender this gesture is most unusual, and it takes Antonio by surprise. Despite Bassanio's reluctance to let his friend enter into the agreement, Antonio goes ahead with the "merry bond," which involves the forfeiture of a pound of his flesh if he defaults. He feels very confident that his ships will come in well before the due date and supply him with enough money to repay the debt easily (1.3.153–56, 178). Rightly or wrongly, he believes Shylock has had a change of heart; he remarks to Bassanio, "The Hebrew will turn Christian: he grows kind" (175).

Earlier in this scene, when Bassanio invites him to dinner, Shylock rejects the invitation, asserting allegiance to his religion (1.3.30–35). But in act 2 Shylock goes off to dine with Bassanio and his friends after all. His explicit motive, or what he says to

Jessica, is "to feed upon / The prodigal Christian" (2.5.14–15). One can't help suspect, however, that he may still be trying to ingratiate himself further with Antonio, who will be there, too. Whatever the case—and these motives are not mutually exclusive—this is the first indication that Shylock's tie to his religion may not be as strong as it seems, regardless of his knowledge of the Hebrew bible, which he expounds in 1.3, or his membership in a synagogue (3.1.122–23).

Act 2 develops thematically many of the bonds already discussed and introduces others. Portia's suitors, for instance, are bound by the terms of their choice: if they pick the wrong casket, they must leave at once, tell no one about the choice, and remain unwed for life (2.9.10–15). During the scenes with the princes of Morocco and Arragon, Portia also shows the obligations of courtesy, and only after they leave does she reveal her true feelings toward them, which are just as unfavorable as those toward her earlier suitors (1.2.38–108, 2.7.79, 2.9.78–79). Lancelot Gobbo's monologue in 2.2 comically develops the motif of the bond between master and servant, which is further developed in Shylock's attitude toward him (2.5.45–50; cp. 1.3.172–73). These ties are not indissoluble; nevertheless, they require some searching of one's conscience to break them.

Act 3 dramatizes the breaking of some bonds and the forging of new ones. Word arrives that one of Antonio's ships has been lost. Meantime, Jessica has eloped with Lorenzo, and Shylock mourns his daughter and his ducats (2.8.12–22, 3.1.23–35, 75–91). When, after mocking Shylock's despair, Salarino mentions Antonio's ill fortune, he (more or less inadvertently) ignites Shylock's desire for revenge, which he justifies in his long speech identifying himself, as a Jew, with all humanity, including Christians (3.1.55–69). His claim that Christians have taught him to be vindictive may be arguable, but neither Salarino nor Solanio disputes the claim, interrupted though they are at this point by a messenger summoning them to Antonio's house. The scene concludes as Shylock, receiving unwelcome news of Jessica's spendthrift ways from Tubal, pledges to exact his forfeit if Antonio defaults on his debt payment.

While this is going on in Venice, at Belmont Portia and Bassanio enjoy an idyllic time together and have fallen in love. It is questionable whether Portia's clear preference for Bassanio leads her to assist him in making the right choice of caskets by having a song sung, whose first three lines rhyme with *lead* (3.2.63–65). She overtly insists that though she is tempted to aid Bassanio, she will not (3.2.10–12), and some critics take her at her word. Nevertheless, it is only here, in Bassanio's casket scene and not in the others, that any music is played. Has Portia thus violated her bond? Bassanio, of course, may be too engrossed in meditation while the song is sung, pondering the inscriptions on the caskets and making his decision. When at length he chooses the right casket, Portia is overjoyed, as everyone else is, and Graziano and Nerissa also announce their engagement. So the bonds of matrimony are forged, sealed by the rings that Portia and Nerissa give their husbands.

Into this scene of festivity intrudes the news from Venice, that Antonio's ships have all been lost and he is forfeit to Shylock. Bassanio is stunned, but Portia leaps to his aid as a good, rich wife should, sending him immediately back to Venice with more than enough ducats to satisfy the debt Antonio owes. She only insists that they be married first, without taking any time to consummate the act. After Bassanio and Graziano leave, she turns her household over to Lorenzo and Jessica (3.4.24–40), who have come to Belmont with Salerio bearing the ill tidings, and she announces her plan to Nerissa to follow their husbands to Venice disguised as men (3.4.57–84). Violating the propriety of their sex by doing so, they are bound to a higher obligation—to help their loved ones where and as they can.

Act 3, scene 3 is a prelude to the trial scene (4.1), showing Shylock's adamant refusal to relinquish his hold on Antonio. He stands on Venetian justice, he claims, which cannot allow any divergence without risking its credit in the world. Antonio concedes as much (3.3.26–29), as later the duke does, too. A state is bound to observe and enforce its laws, as Shylock well knows. He thus appears to have the upper hand here and during the first part of 4.1. When Portia appears in disguise as a doctor of laws with Nerissa as her clerk, she recognizes the justice of Shylock's claim at first and pleads with him to show mercy. But Shylock feels no compulsion to be merciful, whereupon Portia argues that the quality of mercy is not "strained," or forced (4.1.181–202). Men are not bound to be merciful; mercy issues from a generous and forgiving spirit. Her words fall on deaf ears, unfortunately, and Shylock proceeds with his claim to exact his forfeit.

Just as he is about to do so, despite the pleas from all concerned,

Bassanio choosing the casket; illustration by Gordon Browne in *The Works of Shakespeare*, ed. Henry Irving and Frank A. Marshall (1888), vol. 3.

Portia interrupts him with another piece of Venetian law about which Shylock is unaware. The moment resembles that in Genesis, when Abraham, having bound his son Isaac as a sacrifice to the Lord, is interrupted by an angel and prevented from going through with his act of human sacrifice, which is so adverse to everything Judaism stands for (see Gen. 22.1–14). By her action, Portia not only saves Antonio's life, she also saves Shylock from violating his own humanity by performing an extremely cruel, not to say inhuman, deed. Only she does not stop there. Caught in a web of his own making, Shylock then tries to leave with the money Bassanio has offered him, but he is not allowed to receive so much as his principal. The law, which Shylock has insisted he is bound to, has yet another hold on him: as an alien in Venice (Jews were not allowed to be citizens), his life and all his possessions are forfeit to the state, insofar as he had designs against the life of a true Venetian citizen.

Here the duke's mercy is spontaneous, contrasting directly with Shylock's refusal earlier to show any mercy at all. Antonio's mercy is more considered and deliberate, and for modern audiences more problematical. First, Shylock must agree to bequeath all he possesses at his death to Lorenzo and Jessica; second, he must convert to Christianity. A careful reading of the play will show that however difficult Shylock finds these conditions, they are not impossible. For he has not been a truly religious Jew. He has not been deeply bound to his religion, for no Jew would insist on such diabolical vengeance as Shylock has done. That is why when he enters the duke's court (4.1.14), he enters alone. Neither Tubal nor any other member of the Jewish community in Venice accompanies him. (In the National Theatre's production in London in 1999, Tubal does enter but leaves when he sees Shylock determined to go through with his action against Antonio.) His forced conversion may repel us today, though it probably did not repel Shakespeare's audience, who may have seen this as Shylock's best chance for salvation. Nevertheless, Shylock's pain at the end, and his admission that he is ill, leaves many on stage and off feeling uncomfortable.

The last act is important for restoring the play to something more closely resembling romantic comedy. The main action involves the rings that Portia and Nerissa, in their disguises, have extracted from their husbands. Despite the men's promises never

Graziano giving Portia the ring; illustration by Gordon Browne in *The Works of Shakespeare*, ed. Henry Irving and Frank A. Marshall (1888), vol. 3.

to part with the rings, at Antonio's urging Bassanio yields and sends Graziano after Portia with his ring (4.1.445–50). We do not see how Nerissa gets the ring from Graziano, who shows her the way to Shylock's house to deliver his deed of gift to Lorenzo and Jessica, but it is she who first denounces her husband for having given the ring away (5.1.141–65). What follows is an object lesson to the husbands, teaching them to respect more completely the vows they make to their wives and, by implication, all of the bonds that unite them as husband and wife. By accepting Antonio's pledge of his soul to guarantee Bassanio's honor, Portia also establishes the priorities she feels are necessary for her future household.

CONCLUSION

Like any literary artifact, a Shakespearean play is a complex structure that uses a variety of techniques. Thematic and dramatic structures, including verse patterns, prose, imagery and metaphor, characters, theatrical conventions, multiple plots, and the juxta-position of scenes—each contributes to the overall design and meaning of the play. Close reading and analysis of these patterns lead to a richer and fuller experience, bringing us ever closer to the heart of Shakespeare's work. In addition, analysis of Shake-speare's source materials and of the ways in which he adapts them to his own purposes also helps bring us closer. Because Shake-speare's works are as complex as they are, involving ambiguities that reflect the profound depths of human experience, analysis and discussion may seem endless, but the deeper one probes, the more fruitful the results.

QUESTIONS FOR WRITTEN AND ORAL DISCUSSION

1. Discuss questions of genre that *The Merchant of Venice* raises. What elements of tragedy does it include? What are its comic aspects? Is Shylock a tragic victim or a comic villain, like Marlowe's Barabas?

2. The modern critic Northrop Frye says that in a well-constructed comedy not all of the moods are comic in the sense of festive. He also says that in comedy not all of the characters advance toward the new society of the final scene; a character or two remain isolated from this action like spectators of it. In *The Merchant of Venice* who fits this description? Is it important that such characters should be included in comedy, and if so, why?

3. Another critic, John Baxter, says that Shakespeare reveals "a complex awareness of life." What do you think he means by that? What are the identifiable components of this non-simplistic view of life in *The Merchant of Venice*, and how are they developed?

4. Analyze carefully as a piece of poetry Portia's speech on the quality of mercy (4.1.181–99). What are the principal poetic devices that she uses? How, for example, is mercy like a "gentle rain"? What biblical allusions does she employ, and how do they operate in her speech? Do the same thing for other set speeches in this play.

5. Analyze Shylock's prose speech at 3.1.50–69. How does his use of rhetorical questions work? What effect do his repetitions or parallelisms have? How powerful is the speech, and to what do you attribute its overall effectiveness?

6. Organize a debate about the song, "Tell me where is fancy bred" (3.2.63–72) as Bassanio decides which casket to choose. Have one side argue that Portia unfairly leads Bassanio to make the right choice, because she has fallen in love with him. Have the other side argue that the song is a harmless interlude used simply to vary the casket-choosing episode; moreover, Portia has already explicitly said that she will not teach Bassanio how to choose (3.2.10–12) and that if he loves her, he will choose correctly (2.2.41).

7. What is Shylock's motive at 4.1.84–86 for rejecting the money offered him and insisting on the forfeit of the bond? When the moneylender is frustrated in his attempt to kill the merchant, why does Shakespeare continue the episode, bringing in additional penalties against Shylock, including the requirement that he convert to Christianity?

8. Find as many biblical allusions as you can in *The Merchant of Venice*. How does each one function in its context? Why, for example, does Shylock recount the story of Jacob and Laban to Antonio in 1.3? What

effect does it have? Do the names of the Jewish characters—Jessica, Tubal, Chus (who is mentioned but does not appear), as well as Shylock—carry any special significance, given their biblical origins?

9. What is Graziano's dramatic function in *The Merchant of Venice?* He is Shakespeare's invention, not found in any of his sources. So is Nerissa. What does their relationship add to the development of the play, thematically as well as dramatically?

10. How do Venice and Belmont contrast with each other? In what sense is Belmont a pastoral retreat from the world, especially the world of business, lawsuits, politics, and the like?

11. Organize another debate on the issue of Christian anti-Semitism in the play. Is it adequate grounds for Shylock's revenge? Or does Shylock go too far? What about his conversion to Christianity? Is Antonio justified in making this a condition of Shylock's reprieve?

12. Write a sixth act to *The Merchant of Venice* in modern English about the married life of Portia and Bassanio, Nerissa and Graziano, Jessica and Lorenzo. How do you imagine they get on with each other? Where do Shylock and Antonio fit in, or do they? Do they become friends at last?

SUGGESTED READINGS

Barber, C. L. *Shakespeare's Festive Comedy*. Princeton, NJ: Princeton University Press, 1959.

Bloom, Harold. *Shakespeare: The Invention of the Human*. New York: Riverhead Books, 1998.

Danson, Lawrence. *The Harmonies of "The Merchant of Venice."* New Haven, CT: Yale University Press, 1978.

Goddard, Harold. *The Meaning of Shakespeare*. 2 vols. Chicago, IL: Phoenix Books, 1951.

Leggatt, Alexander. *Shakespeare's Comedies of Love*. London: Methuen, 1974.

Lyon, John. *The Merchant of Venice*. Twayne's New Critical Introductions to Shakespeare. Boston, MA: Twayne, 1988.

Mahood, M. M. Critical introduction to *The Merchant of Venice*. Cambridge: Cambridge University Press, 1987.

2

Venice and Its Treatment of Jews

The city of Venice in coastal northern Italy was famous in Shakespeare's day. It had the reputation of great wealth ("Venice the Rich"), political wisdom ("Venice the Wise"), impartial justice ("Venice the Just"), and liberalism, in sexual mores as in much else ("Venice the Gallant"). All of these attributes contributed to the idea, or "myth," of Venice as it was known and regarded in the sixteenth century throughout Europe. Travelers from England to the Continent going as far as Italy invariably sought out Venice for at least a few days' residence, though usually much longer. Englishmen, like Thomas Coryat and Fynes Moryson in the early seventeenth century, have left long and detailed accounts of their visits. The myth of Venice was so powerful that it inspired not only Shakespeare but his great contemporary Ben Jonson as well.

The various aspects of the myth may be explained thus: "Venice the Rich" refers to the great wealth that Venice accumulated over the centuries through its trade with the East. Its opulence was symbolized by the riches held in the Treasury of Saint Mark, which contained an abundance of gold, precious stones such as diamonds, rubies, and emeralds, and elaborate artifacts of both gold and silver. To maintain its trade and protect its wealth, Venice of course developed a powerful military force; its famous Arsenal made visible for all to see (like today's military parades) how great

View of Venice, from *Civitatis Orbis Terrarum* (1593), by Georg Braun and Frans Hogenburg. Reproduced courtesy of The Folger Shakespeare Library.

this force was. Its huge arms factory could outfit a large galleon in a single day.

"Venice the Wise" derived from the republic's reputation for political wisdom. As a republic it had endured for centuries, much to the amazement of those living under monarchical rule, like the English. It had never been conquered, testimony to the patriotism of its citizenry, who enjoyed greater liberty than most others. Related to this aspect of the myth was "Venice the Just." Its justice was conservative and often severe, but also impartial, since nobles and commoners, citizens and aliens, were all equally protected under its laws, a point stressed in *The Merchant of Venice*.

What most attracted visitors to Venice, however, was doubtless its standing as the pleasure capital of Europe ("Venice the Gallant"). Revelries—for example, the masques and music that annoy Shylock in act 2—were among the many pleasures tourists could enjoy. Other entertainments abounded: Venice was perhaps most famous for its many courtesans, women richly dressed and beautiful to behold. The physical attraction of Venice was also extremely appealing. The magnificent palazzos that bordered the Grand Canal, combined with the beautiful canals, bridges, and churches (to say nothing of the art works they contained), made up a good part of the splendor the city projected.

Of course, like anything else, the reality and the myth were in some ways at variance. By the end of the sixteenth century, Venice was already in decline as a mercantile giant, thanks to the Portuguese navigators who had found an alternative route around Africa for trade with the East, the main source of Venice's wealth for centuries. While its liberal reputation was deserved, it had its dark side, too, in the licentiousness for which the city was also famous, or infamous. The authorities, moreover, discouraged the citizens from much contact with foreigners. Though its justice was impartial, it was also rigorous. Persons could be sent to the galleys for what today would be regarded as the slightest legal infraction. Swearing could be punished with the loss of a hand, tongue, or eye, for example, and corruption among the judges was notorious.

Nevertheless, Venice as the pleasure capital and its position in Europe as a rich mercantile center attracted thousands of tourists, who believed enough of the myth to come and visit the city to see it for themselves. They became a major source of income, then as now. Its commercial enterprise and its reputation for liberty and justice also attracted a large community of Jews, who lived in what was the first ghetto in Europe, founded in 1516. (*Ghetto* is the Italian for foundry; the place where the Jews were forced to live as a despised people was the site of an abandoned foundry.) From the mid- and late-thirteenth century, Jewish loan bankers had begun to migrate from Germany, where persecution was rampant, and from central and southern Italy, where Sicily, for example, had expelled the Jews. Since the beginning of the Crusades, in fact, Jews had been persecuted throughout Europe, were thrown out of countries like England and France, and were in constant danger of losing their lives or possessions. Some came to Venice, followed later by emigrants from Spain and Portugal driven out by the Inquisition, which relentlessly persecuted anyone who refused to convert to Christianity. The image of the Wandering Jew thus became a reality, as Jews sought sanctuary wherever they could find it. Venice was one such place where, despite severe restrictions, they could live in relative peace and security. But it was not until the last quarter of the sixteenth century that Jews were well settled there, contributing significantly to the exorbitant taxes imposed on them as a whole—again, as a penalty for remaining infidels, that is, people who refused to accept salvation through Christianity and therefore were aliens who could not become citizens.

The Venetian ghetto, the only place in the city where Jews were permitted to reside, was like a fortress. It served both to protect Jews from depredations of violence and plunder by riotous anti-Semites and to separate them from their Christian neighbors, lest fraternizing should lead to intermarriage, which was forbidden, or conversion to Judaism, which was considered even worse. The ghetto had a single entrance, guarded by police who also enforced the nightly curfew. Overcrowded, the ghetto became squalid and disagreeable, all of which emphasized the inferiority of Jews to Christians. Jews were also compelled to wear distinguishing clothes, such as red or yellow badges and hats. Caught outside the ghetto after curfew, they were subject to fines and imprisonment. In many ways, the ghetto anticipated modern concentration camps and racial discrimination. But because of their highly useful economic function as bankers to the poor, taxpayers, creditors to the state and to individuals, the Jews in Venice were tolerated as a segregated minority and protected by the government. For these reasons, the repeated demands for their expulsion dwindled after 1573 and effectively disappeared by 1580.

Despite the discrimination against them and the limitations on their ability to earn a living—as elsewhere in Europe, they were not permitted to own land or engage in many crafts—Jews prospered in Venice. Unlike London, Venice allowed them to practice their religion openly; several foreign visitors published accounts of visits to their synagogues. On the whole, then, Jews in Venice were treated better than they were in most places. They lived there in peace and could expect, and get, freedom from tyranny and violence. They could also get justice from "Venice the Just," where foreigners (Jews were aliens there, too) as well as citizens had equal rights before the law. That is the basis for Shylock's appeal to the duke, which Antonio—a "royal merchant" and respected magnifico recognizes—himself.

JEWS AND VENETIAN LIFE IN 1581

The first excerpt, extracted from Laurence Aldersey's account of his visit to Venice in 1581, briefly describes the position of Jews in Venice and their customs, including worship in their synagogues. This excerpt clearly illustrates the anti-Semitic attitudes prevalent at the time. Aldersey analyzes the governmental structure of Venice, noting the severe limitations upon the power of the duke, or doge, as he was called. He is not nearly as powerful as the duke in Shakespeare's *Merchant of Venice* appears to be, his authority being well circumscribed by the laws of Venice, which was and remained for a long time the most democratic city-state in Europe. Aldersey's description of women in Venice is also far from flattering but suggests the great wealth Venetians enjoyed, even among working people.

FROM LAURENCE ALDERSEY'S ACCOUNT OF VENICE (1581), IN
RICHARD HAKLUYT'S *PRINCIPAL NAVIGATIONS, VOYAGES,
TRAFFIQUES, AND DISCOVERIES OF THE ENGLISH NATION* (1599)
(12 vols.; Glasgow: James MacLehose and Sons, 1903–5, 5.204–6)

The number of Jews is there thought to be 1,000, who dwell in a certain place of the city and have also a place to which they resort to pray, which is called the Jews' Synagogue. They all and their offspring use to wear red caps (for so they are commanded) because there they may be known from other men. For my further knowledge of these people, I went into their synagogue upon a Saturday, which is their Sabbath day, and I found them in their service or prayers, very devout. They receive the five books of Moses and honor them by carrying them about their church, as papists do their cross.

Their synagogue is in form round and the people sit around it, and in the midst there is a place for him that reads to rest. As for their apparel, all of them wear a large white lawn over their garments [i.e., the tallith, or prayer shawl], which reaches from their head down to the ground.

The Psalms they sing as we do, having no image nor using any manner of idolatry. Their error is that they believe not in Christ, nor yet receive the New Testament. This city of Venice is very fair and greatly to be commended, wherein is good order for all things, and also is very strong and populous. It stands upon the main sea and has many islands about it that belong to it.

To tell you of the duke of Venice and of the Seignory: There is one chosen that ever bears the name of duke, but in truth he is but servant to the Seignory, for of himself he can do little: it is no otherwise with him than with a priest that is at mass upon a festival day, which putting on his golden garment seems to be a great man, but if any man come unto him and crave some friendship at his hands, he will say, "You must go to the masters of the parish, for I cannot pleasure you otherwise than by preferring of your suit." And so it is with the duke of Venice, if any man having a suit come to him and make his complaint and deliver his supplication, it is not for him to help him, but he will tell him, "You must come this day or that day, and then I will prefer your suit to the Seignory and do you the best friendship that I may." Furthermore, if any man bring a letter unto him, he may not open it but in the presence of the Seignory, and they are to see it first, which being read perhaps they will deliver it to him, perhaps not. Of the Seignory there be about three hundred and about forty of the Privy Council of Venice, who usually are arrayed in gowns of crimson satin or crimson damask when they sit in council.

In the city of Venice no man may wear a weapon, except he be a soldier for the Seignory or a scholar of Padua or a gentleman of great countenance, and yet he may not do that without license.

As for the women of Venice, they be rather monsters than women. Every shoemaker's or tailor's wife will have a gown of silk and one to carry up her train, wearing their shoes very near half a yard high from the ground. If a stranger meet one of them, he will surely think by the state that she goes with that he meets a lady.

THOMAS CORYAT'S IMPRESSIONS OF SEVENTEENTH-CENTURY VENICE AND JEWISH LIFE

One of those "strangers" who visited Venice was the Englishman Thomas Coryat (1577?–1617). Although he attended Oxford University, he left without taking a degree. After several years of aimless living and after his father's death in 1607, he embarked on travels to the continent of Europe, mainly on foot. He recorded his impressions in a journal which, after being rejected often, was finally published in 1611 in a volume of nearly 800 pages, including illustrations of copper and steel engravings. It sold well and became a useful travel guide. In 1612 he resumed traveling, this time as far as Turkey, Asia Minor, Egypt, the Holy Land, Persia, and India. Some of his letters home to friends were published in 1616, with a frontispiece of Coryat riding on an elephant. He died in India in 1617. His writings are some of the best accounts of how Venice and other places struck an educated Englishman in the the early seventeenth century, or soon after the composition of *The Merchant of Venice*. Through his detailed and vivid descriptions of Venice, one can picture the Venice of Shakespeare and Jonson's plays, comparing both the "myth" and the settings for the plays with the reality that Coryat presents. Note particularly his description of the Rialto (the square, not the bridge), where the merchants gathered, as well as his account of the Jews he met during his visit to their synagogue in the ghetto. Keep in mind that his prejudice toward Jews is typical of the time.

FROM THOMAS CORYAT, *CORYAT'S CRUDITIES* (1611)
(2 vols.; reprint, Glasgow: James MacLehose and Sons, 1905, vol.1:
"Observations of Venice," 301–428 [Page references are to the
reprint])

The first place of Venice that was inhabited, is that which now they call the Rialto, which word is derived from rivus altus, that is, a deep river, because the water is deeper there than about the other islands. And the first that dwelt in the same Rialto was a poor man called Joannes Bonus, who got his living there by fishing. After this many repaired unto this man's house for the safety of their lives in the time of Radagisus, King of the Goths, who with a huge army of two hundred thousand men invaded Italy, wasting it extremely with fire and sword. (pp. 304–5)

• • •

The city is divided in the midst by a goodly fair channel [canal], which they call Canal il Grande. The same is crooked, and made in the form of a Roman *S*. It is in length a thousand and three hundred paces, and in breadth at least forty, in some places more. The six parts of the city whereof Venice consisteth are situate on both sides of this Canal il Grande. The names of them are these: St. Marco, Castello, Canareio, that lie on one side of it, and those on the other side are called St. Polo, St. Croce, Dorso Duro. Also both sides of this channel are adorned with many sumptuous and magnificent palaces that stand very near to the water and make a very glorious and beautiful show. For many of them are of a great height, three or four stories high, most being built with brick, and some few with fair free stone. Besides, they are adorned with a great multitude of stately pillars made partly of white stone and partly of Istrian marble. Their roofs too much differ from those of our English buildings. For they are all flat and built in that manner as men may walk upon them, as I have often observed. (p. 306)

• • •

[I]t is said there are in the city of Venice at the least a hundred and twenty goodly palaces, the greatest part whereof are built upon the sides of this great channel. So that if you will take a view of the fairest palaces that the whole city yieldeth, you must behold these palaces of the Canal il Grande, either from the Rialto bridge, or passing in a little boat which they call a gondola . . . through the channel itself. For this place present-eth the most glorious buildings of all Venice, saving the Duke's Palace that adjoineth to St. Mark's Church, and some other magnificent fronts of St. Mark's Street. (p. 308)

• • •

There is only one bridge to go over the great channel, which is the same that leadeth from St. Mark's to the Rialto and joineth together both the banks of the channel. This bridge is commonly called Ponte de Rialto and is the fairest bridge by many degrees for one arch that ever I saw, read, or heard of. . . . Truly, the exact view hereof ministered unto me no small matter of admiration to see a bridge of that length (for it is two hundred foot long, as the channel being at the least forty paces broad, as I have written) so curiously compacted together with only one arch. . . . It was first built with timber (as I heard divers Venetian gentlemen report), but because that was not correspondent to the magnificence of the other parts of the city, they defaced that and built this most sumptuous bridge with squared white stone, having two fair rows of pretty little houses for artificers, which are only shops, not dwelling houses. Of these shops there are two rows in each side of the bridge until you come to the top, on the other side towards the Rialto twelve ascents. (pp. 309–10)

• • •

There are in Venice thirteen ferries or passages, which they commonly call *traghetti*, where passengers may be transported in a gondola to what place of the city they will. Of which thirteen, one is under the Rialto bridge. But the boatmen that attend at this ferry are the most vicious and licentious varlets [Knaves] about the city. For if a stranger entereth into one of their gondolas and doth not presently tell them whither he will go, they will incontinently carry him of their own accord to a religious house [an obvious euphemism] forsooth, where his plumes shall be well pulled before he cometh forth again. . . . Therefore I counsel all my countrymen whatsoever, gentlemen or others that determine hereafter to see Venice, to beware of the Circean cups and the Sirens' melody, I mean these seducing and tempting gondoliers of the Rialto bridge, lest they afterward cry *Peccavi* ["You were doing wicked things!"] when it is too late. (p. 311)

• • •

The Rialto, which is at the farther side of the bridge as you come from St. Mark's, is a most stately building, being the Exchange of Venice, where the Venetian gentlemen and the merchants do meet twice a day, betwixt eleven and twelve of the the clock in the morning, and betwixt five and six of the clock in the afternoon. The Rialto is of a goodly heighth, built all with brick as the palaces are, adorned with many fair walks or open galleries that I have afore mentioned and hath a pretty quadrangular court adjoining to it. But it is inferior to our Exchange in London, though indeed there is a far greater quantity of building in this than in ours. In one of the higher rooms which belongeth only to the State, there is kept wondrous abundance of treasure. . . .

Each street hath many several bridges, some more, some less, whereof most are stony, and those vaulted with one arch. The whole number of them is said to be four hundred and fifty. (p. 312)

• • •

I was at a place where the whole fraternity of the Jews dwelleth together, which is called the *ghetto*, being an island: for it is enclosed round about with water. It is thought there are of them in all betwixt five and six thousand. They are distinguished and discerned from the Christians by their habits on their heads; for some of them do wear hats and those red—only those Jews that are born in the western parts of the world, as in Italy, etc.; but the eastern Jews being otherwise called the Levantine Jews, which are born in Jerusalem, Alexandria, Constantinople, etc., wear turbans upon their heads as the Turks do. But the difference is this: the Turks wear white, the Jews yellow. By that word turban I understand a roll of fine linen instead of hats, whereof many have been often worn by the Turks in London. They have divers synagogues in their ghetto, at the least seven, where all of them, both men, women, and children do meet together upon their Sabbath, which is Saturday, to the end to do their devotion and to serve God in their kind, each company having a several synagogue. In the midst of the synagogue they have a round seat made of wainscot, having eight open spaces therein, at two whereof which are at the sides, they enter into the seat as by doors. The Levite that readeth the Law to them hath before him at the time of divine service an exceeding long piece of parchment rolled up upon two wooden handles, in which is written the whole sum and contents of Moses law in Hebrew: that doth he (being discerned from the lay people only by wearing of a red cap, whereas the others do wear red hats) pronounce before the congregation not by a sober, distinct, and orderly reading, but by an exceeding loud yelling, indecent roaring, and as it were a beastly bellowing of it forth. And that after such a confused and huddling manner that I think the hearers can very hardly understand him. . . . Amongst others that are within the room with him, one is he that cometh purposely thither from his seat to the end to read the law and pronounce some part of it with him; who when he is gone, another riseth from his seat and cometh thither to supply his room. This order they keep from the beginning of service to the end. One custom I observed amongst them very irreverent and profane, that none of them, either when they enter the synagogue or when they sit down in the places, or when they go forth again, do any reverence or obeisance, answerable to such a place of worship of God, either by uncovering their heads, kneeling, of any other external gesture, but boldly dash into the room with their Hebrew books in their hands, and presently sit in their places without any more ado. Every one of them whatsoever he be, man or child, weareth a kind of light yellowish veil [i.e., a prayer shawl] made of linsey-woolsey (as I take it) over his shoulders, something worse than our coarser holland, which reacheth a little beneath the middle of their backs. They have a great company of candlesticks in each synagogue made partly of glass and partly of brass and pewter, which hang square about their synagogue. For in that form is their synagogue built. Of their candlesticks I told above sixty in the same synagogue.

I observed some few of those Jews, especially some of the Levantines, to be such goodly and proper men, that then I said to myself our English proverb: To look like a Jew (whereby is meant sometimes a weather-beaten warp-faced fellow, sometimes a frenetic and lunatic person, sometimes one discontented) is not true. For indeed I noted some of them to be most elegant and sweet featured persons, which gave me occasion the more to lament their religion. For if they were Christians, then could I better apply unto them that excellent verse of the poet than I can now:

Gratior est pulchro veniens é corpore virtus.

In the room where they celebrate their divine service, no women sit but have a loft or gallery proper to themselves only, where I saw many Jewish women, whereof some were as beautiful as ever I saw, and so gorgeous in their apparel, jewels, and chains of gold, and rings adorned with precious stones, that some of our English countesses do scarce exceed them, having marvelous long trains like princesses that are born up by waiting women serving for the same purpose: an argument to prove that many of the Jews are very rich. . . . They are very religious in two things only, and no more, in that they worship no images, and that they keep their Sabbath so strictly that upon that day they will neither buy nor sell, nor do any secular, profane, or irreligious exercise (I would to God our Christians would imitate the Jews herein), no, not so much as dress their victuals, which is always done the day before, but dedicate themselves wholly to the strict worship of God. Their circumcision they observe as duly as they did any time betwixt Abraham (in whose time it was first instituted) and the incarnation of Christ. For they do circumcise every male child when he is eight days old with a stony knife. But I had no opportunity to see it. Likewise they keep many of those ancient feasts that were instituted by Moses. Amongst the rest the Feast of Tabernacles is very ceremoniously observed by them. From swine's flesh they abstain as their ancient forefathers were wont to do, in which the Turks do imitate them to this day. Truly, it is a most lamentable case for a Christian to consider the damnable estate of these miserable Jews, in that they reject the true Messiah and Savior of their souls, hoping to be saved rather by the observation of these Mosaical ceremonies (the date whereof was fully expired at Christ's incarnation) than by the merits of the Savior of the world, without whom all mankind shall perish. And as pitiful as it is to see that few of them living in Italy are converted to the Christian religion. For this I understand is the main impediment to their conversion: All their goods are confiscated as soon as they embrace Christianity. And this I heard is the reason: because whereas many of them do raise their fortunes by usury, in so much that they do not only shear, but also flay many a poor Christian's estate by their griping extortion, it is therefore decreed by the Pope and other free princes in whose territories they live, that they shall make a restitution of all their ill gotten goods, and so disclog their souls and consciences when they are admitted by holy baptism into the bosom of Christ's church. Seeing when their goods are taken from them at their conversion they are left even naked, and destitute of their means of maintenance, there are fewer Jews converted to Christianity in Italy than in any country of Christendom. Whereas in Germany, Poland, and other places, Jews that are converted (which doth often happen, as Emanuel Tremellius was converted in Germany) do enjoy their estates as they did before. (pp. 370–74)

• • •

I was at one of [the Venetian] playhouses where I saw a comedy acted. The house is very beggarly and base in comparison of our stately playhouses in England: neither can their actors compare with us for apparel, shows, and music. Here I observed certain things that I never saw before. For I saw women act, a thing that I never saw before, though I have heard that it hath sometimes been used in London, and they performed it with as good a grace, action, gesture, and whatsoever convenient for a player as I ever saw any masculine actor. Also their noble and famous courtesans came to this comedy, but so disguised that a man cannot perceive them. For they wore double masks upon their faces, to the end they might not be seen: one reaching from the top of their forehead to their chin and under their neck; another with twists of downy or woolly stuff covering their noses. And as for their necks round about, they were so covered and wrapped with cobweb lawn and other things, that no part of their skin could be discerned. Upon their heads they wore little black felt caps very like to those of the clarissimos. . . . Also each of them wore a black short taffeta cloak. They were so graced that they sat on high alone by themselves in the best room of all the playhouse. If any man should be so resolute to unmask one of them but in merriment only to see their faces, it is said that were he never so noble or worthy a personage, he should be cut to pieces before he should come forth of the room, especially if he were a stranger. I saw some men also in the playhouse disguised in the same manner with double visors; those were said to be the favorites of the same courtesans. They sit not here in galleries as we do in London, for there is but one or two little galleries in the house, wherein the courtesans only sit. But all the men do sit beneath the yard or court, every man upon his several stool, for which he payeth a gazet [i.e., about an English penny]. (pp. 386–87)

• • •

Now whereas the Venetian ducat is much spoken of, you must consider that this word *ducat* doth not signify any one certain coin. But many several pieces do concur to make one ducat, namely six livers and two gazets, which do countervail four shillings and eight pence of our money. So that a ducat is sometimes more, sometimes less. (p. 423)

FYNES MORYSON'S ACCOUNTS OF HIS TRAVELS

Another educated Englishman who visited Venice and left an excellent account of his travels is Fynes Moryson (1566–1630). Always wanting to travel, he sailed in 1591 for Europe, where he spent the next six years wandering around the Continent. He visited the cities of northern Italy from April 1584 to the beginning of 1595, returning to England in May. In December he was off again, this time with his younger brother, Henry, and they traveled as far as the Holy Land. During this trip Henry died (4 July 1596) in a village near Antioch. Fynes returned to England via Constantinople, Venice, and Stade in 1597. In 1606, he began writing up his travels. But the account proved so bulky that he destroyed it and began a briefer record of his experiences. The first three parts were entered in the Stationers' Register in 1617 under the title of "An Itinerary," but the next two parts remained in manuscript for many years. A large portion of this voluminous work was published as *Shakespeare's Europe* in 1903; the whole of the 1617 edition was reissued in 1907–8 in Glasgow in four volumes. Both the *Itinerary* and *Shakespeare's Europe*, extracts from which follow, complement Coryat's views of Europe and especially Venice. Like Coryat's account, Moryson's works help us to visualize the city and its people and to compare them not only with other Italians, as Moryson does, but with the characters and places found in *The Merchant of Venice*. Notice especially Moryson's description of the magnificoes, comparing them with Antonio and Bassanio, and of the Jews. In the extract from *Shakespeare's Europe* he describes the political system of Venice and the administration of its laws, which again may be compared with Shakespeare's portrayal of them in his play. His attitude toward Jews, like Coryat's, was typical of the time.

FROM FYNES MORYSON, *AN ITINERARY* (1617)
(4 vols.; Glasgow: J. MacLehose and Sons, 1907)

They say the merchants of Florence are crafty, those of Lucca covetous, the Venetians most bold (hazarding all in one ship), those of Milan honest. . . . The Calabrians are said to be officious to strangers in hope of gain, the Neapolitans to love all that excel in any virtue, those of Lucca

to reverence strangers and to defend them from all wrongs. The Florentines to be officious towards them without hope of gain and to com-
municate their fortunes and counsels to them if they stay long there. The
Venetians to be officious in words. (p. 456)

• • •

The Milanese are said to be little jealous and to hate fat women. The
Mantuans to love women that can dance. The Florentines to love a modest woman, and one that loves home. The Neapolitans to love a stately
high-minded woman. Those of Lucca are said to love constantly, the
Venetians contrarily, and to desire fat women with great dugs, but to love
without choice, and to force them if others have enjoyed. The Ferrarians
to hate their rival. Those of Siena to be rapt with fair faces. (p. 457)

• • •

The Neapolitans are said to woo by horsemanship and tilting. Those
of Milan with feasts and by slandering the women that refuse them. Those
of Ferrara by praises. Those of Mantua by masks or dancing. . . . The Venetians by boasting and magnificence. Those of Bologna by gifts. The
Florentines by sonnets. Those of Siena by feigned tears. Those of Lucca
by obstinate loving. Those of Verona by obsequiousness. The Romans
and Aretines by witty jests. (p. 458)

• • •

The women of Lucca are accounted honest and skilful in cookery.
Those of Siena fair and well affected to poets. The Florentines delicate
and good at the needle and matters of the family. . . . The Venetians of a
variable disposition, very jealous, and some of them giving the use of
their bodies freely without reward (but I should think there be few such,
for they pleasantly scoff at our English women, that they give the fruit of
love to their lovers for charity—vulgarly *per amor' di Dio*—as they give
alms to beggars), and affecting to have yellow hair, white skins, and
cherry cheeks, all by art, and to have short legs. And of the Venetian most
famous courtesans it is proverbially said, *Son grasse di stracci, bianche
di calcina, rosse di bellito, alte di zoccole* (They are fat with clouts, white
with chalk, red with painting, and high with shoes). In general, it is said
of the Italian women: *Sono gazze a le porte, santa in chiesa, capre n'i
giardini, diavoli in case, angeli in strada, sirene alla fenestra* (They are
magpies at the door, saints in the church, goats in the garden, devils in
the house, angels in the street, and sirens at the window). (pp. 458–59)

• • •

A GENERAL AND BRIEF DISCOURSE OF THE JEWS

The Jews are a nation incredibly despised among all Christians and of
the Turks also and were dispersed throughout the face of the world, save

that they have been long banished out of some Christian kingdoms, as England and France, and Netherland, where notwithstanding they lurk disguised, though they be but allowed habitation by the state. And where they are allowed to dwell, they live upon usury and selling of frippery wares, as brokers, therein permitted by Christian princes for private gain to use horrible extortions upon the subjects, but are not allowed to buy any lands, houses, or stable inheritances; neither have they any coin of their own but use the coins of princes where they live. The ten tribes of the kingdom of Israel were long since carried captive and dispersed in the furthest East and are not known where they live, having no commerce with the Jews known to us. . . .

Generally, in Poland they live in equal right with Christians, for King Casimir the Great, having a Jew to his concubine (which he was not permitted to marry) gave them great privileges, and this among the rest, that the law might not proceed against a Jew in any action but upon the testimony of Jews. But in Bohemia and Germany, the Jews under the Emperor lived in great oppression and basely condemned by the people being Christians. In Italy likewise the Jews live in no respect, no not the most learned or richest of them, but in less contempt of the people, and the princes who extort upon their own subjects do also for gain admit the Jews into their cities and permit them to use horrible extortion upon their subjects in the lending of money and in selling or in letting out by the day or week upon use both men's and women's apparel and furniture for horses and all kind of frippery wares. Thus at Venice they have a courtyard closed with gates and capable of great numbers wherein they dwell. At Rome they have whole streets allowed for their habitation and live there in great number, paying tribute to the Pope at Shrovetide, when they are allowed to show public games. They are allowed to live in all the cities of Italy and have greater privileges in Piemont than in other parts, but in all these places they are tied to wear a red or yellow cap, or more commonly a little bonnet or hat. (pp. 487–89)

FROM FYNES MORYSON, *SHAKESPEARE'S EUROPE* (1617)
(4 vols.; Glasgow: J. MacLenose, 1907)

The gentlemen of Venice in singularity will be called nobles and appropriate to themselves the title of "clarissimo," for which and their general insolency they are reproved and condemned, not only by strangers (who may as safely stumble upon a bull as upon one of these gentlemen, so as when one of them passed by I have heard men say, *Guardia, il toro*, "Look, or take heed to the bull," as they cry when a bull is baited in the streets), but also by other Italian gentlemen who by writing in the vulgar tongue tax them of unsupportable pride insomuch as (to use their own words) they dream themselves to be dukes and marquises, while they are indeed covetous, miserable, breakers of faith and hateful to all men for their pride, vainglory, and ambition; yea, in the very city they have a proverb: *D'una pietra bianca, d'un nobile Veneziano, et d'una cortigiana ch'abbia madre, Dio ci guarda*: "From a white stone (because it is slippery), from a gentleman of Venice (for their pride), from a courtesan that hath a mother (to teach her to spoil her lovers), God deliver us." No doubt the senators are most grave, just, reverent, and comely persons, and generally they are all rich and many abound in treasure. In Padua, il signor Pio Obici was said to have 12,000 crowns yearly rent, and I was credibly informed that in Brescia divers gentlemen had from ten to thirty thousand crowns yearly rent. And the estates of the gentlemen of Venice must in all probability be much greater. (pp. 152–53)

• • •

THE JUSTICE, LAWS, AND JUDGMENTS IN THE STATE OF VENICE

The Senate of Venice is most reverent for the gray heads, gravity, and comeliness of their persons, and their stately habits, but for nothing more than their strict observing of justice. They have a law that in time of Carnival or Shrovetide, no man that is masked may wear a sword, because being unknown, he might thereby have means to kill his enemy on the sudden; and while I was in Italy, a foreign gentleman upon a fancy to mock the officers of justice, being masked, wore a wooden lath like sword. The officers apprehended him, and finding it to be a lath, yet carried him to the magistrate, who with a grave countenance said to him, *Non burlar' con la giusticia, veh!* ("Jest not with the justice, mark me!"). And he found that he had mocked himself more than the officers, for he paid not a few crowns before he could be freed by mediation of great friends. But since the City of Venice lies open without any walls, so as malefactors may easily escape, and the city lies upon Lombardy, where murders are frequent, the city especially in time of Carnival is much subject to murders and like outrages. And so is the next city, Padua, upon privileges of the university, whereby murder in scholars is punished only by banishment. And that the rather because in the State of Venice (for the great confluence of strangers) it is free for all men to wear arms by the day, excepting pistols, which no man may have without the locks taken off, and also because they who have ill purposes will adventure and use to wear these arms by night also; I say for these reasons murders (especially in the libertine time of Carnival) are frequent in this city, from which also the lesser cities of the state are not free. . . . Adulterers are punished (as other like crimes) according to civil and canon laws, but the Italians impatient to bring their honor under public trials, dispatch the punishment of all jealousies by private revenge, killing not only the men so provoking them, but their wives, sisters, or daughters dishonoring themselves in those kind. Yea, brothers knowing their sisters to be unchaste when they are married, and out of their own house, yet will make this offence known to their husbands, that they may kill them. . . .

Among other high crimes, it is not rare to hear blasphemous speeches in Italy, and the State of Venice is much to be praised for the most severe justice they use against such offenders, having a law to cut out their tongues. (pp. 163–64)

• • •

The laws of Venice in general were reputed so just by the Senate of Nuremburg in Germany as in the year 1508, by ambassadors sent to this state, they obtained a copy of them. Among other civil judgments they give singular justice in cases of debt and have particular judges over merchants bankrupting, who give the creditors security to keep them from prison and cite such bankrupts as fly, selling their goods and dividing them equally among the creditors and preventing all frauds may be used. So if they find other men's goods deposited in their hands, they keep them for their owners. . . .

I have formerly said that all the Venetian laws are made in the Council called *Pregadi*, for when any magistrate judgeth it profitable for the Commonwealth to have any new law made for anything concerning his office and charge, he propounds his reasons in the college of the *Sauij*, and they there being approved, the law is propounded, enacted, and published by the Council *di Pregadi*. So the magistrate of the Pomps (or ceremonies) caused certain sumptuary laws for diet and apparel to be made in this Council which are in force to this day. Yet sometimes the law is made in the Great Council, if the magistrate think that it will receive more life and force by being confirmed therein. (pp. 165–66)

• • •

CUSTOMS

The gentlemen seldom feasting one another, except it be on rare occasions, and those rather particular to some few families than general to all, as upon affinity contracted by marriage; yet to preserve love and acquaintance among them, daily have general meetings in the market places and private in gardens, and to the same end; as also because in many cities they are the chief merchants, they keep the general meetings no less strictly than the merchants of our parts keep their daily meetings at the Exchange, especially at Venice, where the gentlemen daily meet with the merchants before noon on the Rialto, where they stand by themselves, and towards evening in the market place of St. Mark, where they walk together. (p. 459)

WILLIAM THOMAS'S VENETIAN OBSERVATIONS

An earlier traveler to Italy was the Welshman, William Thomas (d. 1554), who became an important Italian scholar. He left his native land in 1544 and spent the next five years abroad, mostly in Italy, where he wrote an Italian primer (1548–49; published 1550) and *The History of Italy* (1549). On his return to England, he became clerk of the king's council, and his opinion was often sought on the principles of government. After Edward VI's death, as a committed Protestant, he strongly opposed the reign of Queen Mary, was tried for treason, and was executed as a traitor in 1554. His *History* gives detailed insights into the workings of the Venetian government, of which he was a close observer, and many other aspects of sixteenth-century Italy, including the position of Jews and the treatment of other aliens.

FROM WILLIAM THOMAS, *THE HISTORY OF ITALY* (1549)
(Ed. George B. Parks. Ithaca, NY: Cornell University Press for the
Folger Shakespeare Library, 1963)

It is almost incredible what gain the Venetians receive by the usury of the Jews, both privately and in common. For in every city the Jews keep open shops of usury, taking gages of ordinary for fifteen in the hundred by the year, and if at the year's end the gage be not redeemed it is forfeit, or at the least done away to a great disadvantage, by reason whereof the Jews are out of measure wealthy in those parts. (p. 69)

• • •

OF DIGNITIES AND OFFICES

They have a Duke, called after their manner *Doge*, who only (amongst all the rest of the nobility) hath his office immutable for term of life, with a certain yearly provision of 4,000 ducats or thereabouts. But that is so appointed unto him for certain ordinary feasts and otherlike charges that his own advantage thereof can be but small. And though in appearance he seemeth of great estate, yet in very deed his power is but small. He keepeth no house, liveth privately, and is in so much servitude that I have heard some of the Venetians themselves call him an honorable slave.

... [In] effect he hath no manner of pre-eminence but the bare honor, the gift of a few small offices, and the liberty *di mettere una parte* [of presenting a motion], which is no more but to propound unto any of the councils his opinion touching the order, reformation, or correction of anything; and that opinion every council is bound to accept into a trial of their sentences by ballot . . . ; and this privilege to have his only opinion balloted no man hath but he. . . .

Next unto the Duke are three called the *Signori Capi* or *Cai*, which outwardly seem inferior to the Duke and yet are of more authority than he. For their power is so absolute that, if there happen cause why, they may arrest the Duke. And all such proclamations as concern the majesty of their commonwealth go forth always under their name: like as we use to say, "In the King's name," so they say, *Da parte dei Signori Cai*. Two of which *Cai*, or one of them with one of the *Avogadori*, have power *di mettere una parte*, such as before rehearsed of the Duke.

They have six counselors of the most worthy among them, who are joined with the Duke to sit in the college for audience of ambassadors and other matters of importance, and these specially are called *la Signoria* [the lordship, or senior cabinet]. . . .

Indeed, *la Signoria* is commonly used as the name of their whole majesty, and principally it doth include the Duke with the rest if the chief officers or senators (to the number of three-score) that accompanieth him when in his solemnity he cometh to church or goeth unto any of the ordinary ceremonies abroad in the city.

Now of such as have authority to consult upon matters of importance (as, we should say, the King's Privy Council), they have seventeen persons appointed called *il Consiglio dei Dieci* [Council of Ten, which counted up to twenty when the Duke and his councilors joined it in regular meetings], of which the Duke, the three *Cai*, and the six counselors are a part. For matters of conclusion of peace, of war, of state, or of otherlike greatest importance, they have a council called *Pregadi* [the invited or elected, actually the Senate, numbering 120], into the which entereth the Duke with the *Consiglio dei Dieci* and of the other principal officers to the number of 200 or thereabouts. (pp. 69–72)

• • •

OF LAWS

Their advocates (as we should say, our men of law) study principally the civil laws [i.e., Roman law] and, besides that, the statutes and customs of the city, which are so many that in manner they suffice themselves. But he that substantially considereth the manner of their proceedings shall plainly see that matters are determined by the judges' consciences and not by the civil nor yet by their own laws. For in every office there be divers judges, and that part that hath most ballots prevaileth ever, be it in matter of debt, of title of land, upon life and death, or otherwise. And in every trial of theft, murder, or such other, the party himself is never suffered to speak. But there be certain advocates waged of the common revenue, which with no less study plead in their defense than the *Avogadori* in the contrary. One day the *Avogadori* cometh into the court and layeth against the felon that either by examination, by torture, or by witness hath been proved, and another day cometh in the advocate and defendeth the felon with the best answer he can devise, so that many time the prisoner tarrieth two, three, and sometime four years ever he come unto his trial of life and death. . . .

Finally, there is a law in Venice that no gentleman Venetian may speak with any ambassador without license of the *Signoria*, for fear of intelligence or of dangerous practice. And because they fear lest civil sedition might be the destruction of their commonwealth, as of divers other it hath been, therefore they have provided an order that when any two gentlemen happen to fall out, either they do so dissemble it that their malice never appeareth to the world or else they agree within themselves. For if it come to the *Signoria*'s knowledge, it cannot be chosen but he that is most faulty receiveth a great rebuke, and many times in those cases divers are banished or sharply punished. As for other laws, though I were sufficiently expert in them, yet partly for briefness and partly because they are not so much necessary to my purpose, I pass them over. But this is clear: there can be no better order of justice in a commonwealth than theirs if it were duly observed. (pp. 76–78)

• • •

THE LIBERTY OF STRANGERS

All men, specially strangers [i.e., foreigners], have so much liberty there that, though they speak very ill by the Venetians, so they attempt nothing in effect against their state no man shall control them for it. And in their *Carnevale* [Carnival] time (which we call Shrovetide) you shall see maskers disguise themselves in the Venetians' habit and come unto their own noses in derision of their customs, their habit, and misery.

Further, he that dwelleth in Venice may reckon himself exempt from subjection. For no man there marketh another's doings, or that meddleth with another man's living. If thou be a papist, there shalt thou want no kind of superstition to feed upon. If thou be a gospeler [Protestant], no man shall ask why thou comest not to church. If thou be a Jew, a Turk, or believest in the devil (so thou spread not thine opinions abroad), thou art free from all controlment. To live married or unmarried, no man shall ask thee why. For eating of flesh in thine own house, what day so ever it be, it maketh no matter. And generally of all other things, so thou offend no man privately, no man shall offend thee, which undoubtedly is one principal cause that draweth so many strangers thither. (p. 83)

QUESTIONS FOR WRITTEN AND ORAL DISCUSSION

1. Describe the "Myth of Venice" as it was understood in Shakespeare's day. In what respects does *The Merchant of Venice* follow the myth, and in what respects does it diverge from it? Is Belmont as Shakespeare renders it part of the myth or separate from Venice?

2. Analyze "Venice the Just" as a specific aspect of the "Myth of Venice." How does Shakespeare simplify the judicial process in act 4 from the actual procedures followed in sixteenth-century Venice? What dramatic values follow from Shakespeare's adaptation of those procedures?

3. The ghetto was the place in Venice in the sixteenth century where all Jews were forced to live, but Shakespeare does not indicate that Shylock and Jessica live there. Can you think of any reasons why he does not place their home in the ghetto? Why does Shakespeare use the setting of Venice at all?

4. Compare Shakespeare's depiction of Venice in *The Merchant of Venice* with Ben Jonson's use of the city in *Volpone*, or with Shakespeare's other Venetian play, *Othello*. What similarities and differences do you find? In which play is Venice portrayed most realistically; that is, which play gives a more concrete and vivid representation of the city, and how is it accomplished?

5. What was synagogue worship like in Venice, as Aldersey and others describe it? At the end of 3.1, Shylock asks Tubal to meet him at their synagogue. Can you imagine Shylock praying in one of the Venetian synagogues as English visitors described them?

6. How powerful does the duke appear in 4.1? Does his power fit the description of the doge of Venice as Aldersey describes him? If not, why does Shakespeare alter his dramatic counterpart in *The Merchant of Venice?* Again, compare *Othello* 1.3, where the duke and his council meet in emergency session.

7. Most visitors today think of the Rialto in Venice as the picturesque bridge over one of the major canals. But the Rialto that Shakespeare refers to in *The Merchant of Venice* is not the bridge. Where is it, and why is it important in the play?

8. What is a *traject*, as Shakespeare uses the term at 3.4.53? Was there such a vessel in sixteenth-century Venice? Compare Coryat's description of the *traghetti*. Would Portia's servant Balthasar have trouble using the traject?

9. How does Coryat describe the Venetian Jews he has seen? Does he

give any clues to the way Shylock should appear in *The Merchant of Venice?* How then should he, Tubal, and Jessica be costumed?

10. Part of act 2 in *The Merchant of Venice* takes place during Carnival season in Venice. How is that season of the year described by English travelers to Venice? Is there any particular reason why Lorenzo chooses it for his elopement with Jessica? What does Shylock think of the carnival, and what does this tell us about his character?

11. Does Fynes Moryson's description of Venetians fit the characters in *The Merchant of Venice?* Or are those characters modeled after Shakespeare's own countrymen and women? What is Moryson's attitude toward the Jews of Venice?

12. How does Moryson describe the legal system of Venice? How does William Thomas? Are there any major differences between them? How do you think they would regard the trial scene in 4.1 of *The Merchant of Venice?* What differences do you find between their descriptions of the criminal justice system in Venice and Shakespeare's dramatization of it?

13. What was the Council of Ten in Venice? Are these the "magnificoes" who enter with the duke at the beginning of 4.1 in *The Merchant of Venice?* What role did they have in sixteenth-century Venice, and how does it compare with their role in Shakespeare's play?

14. Shylock's suit against Antonio is actually a civil suit, and the so-called trial is a hearing, not a criminal trial as such. Why then does Shakespeare make Shylock appeal to the duke for judgment? Why does the the duke resort to Dr. Bellario for help?

15. What kind of justice prevails at the end of 4.1? Is Portia right to demand the strict justice that Shylock has been expecting all along? What kind of mercy does Antonio show? Is it true Christian charity, or some kind of revenge against Shylock?

16. Do you think relations between Jews and Christians have improved by the end of *The Merchant of Venice?* Or will the old antagonism still prevail? What, in fact, has changed? Will Shylock and Antonio now become friends, as Shylock seemed to want at the beginning of the play (e.g., 1.3.133–38)?

17. Are Portia and Nerissa exercising justice in their "ring plot" against their husbands? What are these wives trying to teach their mates? How successful are they, finally?

18. Write a sequel to *The Merchant of Venice* in which Shylock and Antonio meet once more on the Rialto. In another scene, dramatize the relationship between Shylock and Jessica, both now converted Christians. Show, too, how Shylock and his son-in-law Lorenzo interact.

SUGGESTED READINGS

Cardozo Studies in Law and Literature 5 (spring 1993). (A special issue on *The Merchant of Venice* and the legal issues that the play raises.)

Gross, John. *Shylock: Four Hundred Years in the Life of a Legend*. London: Chatto and Windus, 1992.

Jong, Erica. *Serenissima: A Novel of Venice*. New York: Houghton Mifflin, 1987.

McPherson, David C. *Shakespeare, Jonson, and the Myth of Venice*. Newark: University of Delaware Press, 1990.

Shapiro, James. *Shakespeare and the Jews*. New York: Columbia University Press, 1996.

3

Attitudes Toward Jews

After the fall of Jerusalem to the Romans in the first century of the common era and the destruction of the Second Temple, Jews were dispersed throughout the world. Many settled in Europe, North Africa, or elsewhere in the Middle East, though a small remnant remained in what is now Israel. During the first millennium, despite minor outbreaks of violence, Jews generally got along with their neighbors while clinging fast to their own religion and refusing to convert. As Christianity rose and became dominant in Europe, followed by Islam in the Middle East and Africa, Jews continued to live more or less in peace—despite the hostility of the church—until the time of the First Crusade (1095–99). The fervor against infidels that the crusades inspired also provoked an often ferocious anti-Semitism, which led to the destruction of many Jewish communities. The rape, murder, and pillaging of bands of "poor men," led by fanatical priests, became sporadic and widespread across Europe, culminating in the pogroms (massacres) of later centuries and ultimately to the decimation of European Jews in the Holocaust in World War II.

Until 1290, when Edward I expelled all Jews from England, communities of Jewish merchants, craftsmen, and others lived in various parts of the kingdom. As elsewhere in Europe, they were considered aliens and depended on rulers for protection and such rights as they had. They were treated as the sovereign's chattel, or possessions, were heavily taxed, and severely restricted in their way of life. They could not, for instance, own property. Hence, they resorted to what few livelihoods were permitted them, including moneylending, although it is important to remember that not all Jews were moneylenders and not all moneylenders were Jews. Many Jews were poor and served in a variety of capacities, including the most menial occupations. But as nonbelievers in Christ, they were despised by Christians and treated accordingly. They were falsely accused of poisoning wells and causing the plague, and even of ritual murder, despite Pope Innocent IV's bull of 1247, which exonerated them from such charges.

By the end of the thirteenth century, the king of England had exhausted almost all the resources he could get from his Jews in the form of heavy duties, or tallages. He therefore played his last card—expulsion—which pleased the church and allowed him to confiscate all Jewish possessions, including all debts owed to them as moneylenders or pawnbrokers. While some Jews converted to Christianity and lived in the *Domus conversorum* (House of Converts), most fled to other parts of Europe. It was not until the middle of the seventeenth century under the rule of Oliver Cromwell that Jews were officially permitted to return and practice their religion openly in England.

Despite the expulsion edict of 1290, several communities of secret Jews existed in England in the sixteenth century and probably earlier in cities like Bristol and London. Henry VIII had invited Jewish musicians to his court in the early 1500s; the Jewish engineer Joachim Gaunse, or Gans, came to England and helped found the mining industry in Wales. By Shakespeare's time a number of families lived in London and practiced their religion secretly, as recent scholarship has discovered. Many were Marranos, or crypto-Jews, who had come from Spain and Portugal, where under the Catholic Inquisition they were forced to convert to Christianity. Whether Shakespeare knew any Jews—or whether the Dark Lady of the Sonnets was actually a member of the Bassano family, who were Marranos—is not known for certain. What he did know or could hardly avoid knowing was the literary tradition in which Jews were represented.

This tradition did not portray Jews simply as either heroes or villains; it portrayed them as both. In the medieval mystery plays performed by the various trade guilds, the patriarchs of the Old Testament—Abraham, Isaac, and Jacob—and others, like Moses and Daniel, were represented as the venerable personages they were. In the same cycle of plays, villainous Jews, such as Judas Iscariot in the New Testament, were also represented. (Most likely, the representation of Judas in these plays, but especially in medieval paintings, led to the tradition of depicting Jews with red beards and red hair.) From these contrasting conceptions of Jews, a dual image emerged, as the scholar Harold Fisch calls it. On the one hand, the Jew excited "horror, fear, and hatred"; on the other hand, he aroused "wonder, awe, and love" (Fisch 1971, 13). At the same time, Christian theology emphasized the conversion of the Jews as necessary for the Second Coming of Christ. If Jews were shunned as a pariah race, they were also required for ultimate Christian fulfillment, which led to further ambivalence toward them.

As in the earlier mystery plays, on the Elizabethan stage Jews were represented as both heroes and villains. In Robert Wilson's play, *The Three Ladies of London* (1584), for example, the Jew Gerontus appears as the hero, and Mercadore, an Italian merchant, is the comic villain who is willing to convert to Islam rather than pay Gerontus the debt he owes him. In Christopher Marlowe's *The Jew of Malta* (ca. 1588), the Jew Barabas is the villain (see Chapter 1). Interestingly, in 1592, when Marlowe's play was revived by the entrepreneur Philip Henslowe, so was the old play, *An Enterlude of the Vertuous and Godly Queene Hester*, written during the reign of Henry VIII, in which the story of Purim is dramatized and the villain Haman's plot against the Jews is foiled by Ahasuerus's queen, Hester (or Esther).

This double attitude, or dual image, doubtless influenced Shakespeare as he began composing *The Merchant of Venice*. If he was originally inspired by the success of Marlowe's *The Jew of Malta* and moved by the notoriety occasioned by the trial and execution of Roderigo Lopez, a converted Portugese Jew accused of attempting to poison Queen Elizabeth in 1592, he was too much of a humanist and poet to allow such considerations to dominate his conception of Shylock. Not that Shylock is the tragic hero that nineteenth-century critics and actors thought he was. He is the villain of the piece. Shakespeare may at first have conceived him as a comic villain on the order of Barabas, but that conception changed and deepened as the dramatic action progressed. His most famous speech, "Hath not a Jew eyes" (3.1.55 ff.), taken out of context, is often recited as the moving defense of Jews as human beings. But taken in context, it serves Shylock as the justification for his revenge against Antonio, who has long been his enemy (see Chapter 1).

Revenge, of course, was sanctioned by neither religious nor secular authorities; it was vigorously opposed by both. This is one reason that makes Hamlet pause before taking his revenge against Claudius in Shakespeare's tragedy. But throughout the canon of his plays, Shakespeare upholds virtue—"kindness"—against vengeance, as in *As You Like It* (4.3.129) and *The Tempest* (5.1.27–28). Portia pleads with Shylock in the trial scene (4.1) to be merciful, but he is adamant. The elopement of his daughter with a Christian prodigal has been the last straw: he will have his revenge against the Christians by taking the forfeit owed him by Antonio.

Shylock's speeches in 3.1 and later in 4.1 are one way that Shakespeare points up the hypocrisy of the Christians. For in this play, as in Marlowe's *The Jew of Malta*, Christians do not emerge quite as sanctified or as holy as they think they are. The mercy that Antonio shows Shylock at the end of the trial is dubious at best, and modern audiences tend to react negatively to Shylock's forced conversion. But the question then becomes, Why does Shylock become a Christian? In the Jewish religion it is permissible in matters of life and death to break any of the 613 commandments enjoined upon the Israelites, except one—the first commandment of the Decalogue: "Thou shalt have no other gods before me." Before becoming an apostate, a devout Jew would surrender his life.

For all his mouthing of Scripture, Shylock is not a devout Jew, and certainly not a good one. No religious Jew would attempt to carry out the bloodthirsty revenge that Shylock desires against Antonio. The injunction against revenge appears in both the Old and the New Testaments after all (see Lev. 19.17–18, Deut. 32.35, Rom. 12.19, Heb. 10.30); besides, any kind of human sacrifice was anathema to Jews. For this reason, when Shylock appears before the duke and his court in 4.1, he is alone. Not one of his coreligionists—not Tubal or anyone else—joins him in this most crucial occasion of his life. The original stage directions are quite explicit: "Enter Shylock" is all that appears at 4.1.14. Shylock is utterly isolated.

Hal Holbrook as Shylock in a production by The Shakespeare Theatre, directed by Michael Kahn (1999). Photo © Carol Rosegg. Reproduced courtesy of The Shakespeare Theatre.

Unfortunately, in the history of anti-Semitism, Shylock has since become a symbol for a heartless, money-grubbing Jew. Heartless he may be in act 4, but earlier he offers Antonio a loan at no interest in an attempt to win his friendship (1.3.134–37). (Later in act 4 he even rejects Bassanio's offer of twice the value of the bond, 4.1.83). Were he so greedy for money, would he—the money-lender, or usurer—in arranging the loan with Antonio, do the unheard-of thing: demand not one penny in interest? No; instead he refers to the "merry bond" and makes light of the pound of flesh forfeit (1.3.157–67). He seems eager to reconcile with Antonio and to refashion their earlier relationship. All this notwith-standing his opening comment, in an aside, that he hates Antonio "for he is a Christian / But more for . . . / He lends out money gratis and brings down / The rate of usance here with us in Venice" (1.3.39–42). Is this Shylock's ambivalence or Shakespeare's?

The church was ambivalent, too, or at times contradictory in its attitude toward Jews. In his *Tractatus Adversus Iudeos* St. Augustine, on the one hand, attacked Jews severely for rejecting Christ. He saw them as enemies of the church from whom Christians had to be protected. On the other hand, they should be tolerated, he said, because they bore witness to the origins of Christianity and thus, as the custodians of Holy Writ, they vouched for its truth. While expulsions of Jews went on throughout Europe as well as England and especially in Spain and Portugal, the Apostolic See was not consulted, nor did it ever expel Jews from the papal territories. The so-called Augustinian compromise came to an end, nevertheless.

During the Protestant Reformation, Martin Luther, in an early tract, "Christ Was Born a Jew" (1523), argued for better treatment of Jews, certainly if one hoped to convert them to Christianity. But in a later treatise, "On the Jews and Their Lies" (1543), he inveighed against them bitterly, accusing them of obstinacy in refusing to accept conversion and of many other faults, even crimes. In Shakespeare's own time, the theologian Richard Hooker, Bishop Sandys, and others had positive things to say about Jews, however much they deplored their refusal to recognize Christ. In *Of the Laws of Ecclesiastical Polity* (1594), Hooker, in fact, argued that Jewish traditions gave Christians much to emulate and praised their fortitude in the face of oppression. George Sandys's description of Jews recounted in his *Journey* (1610) is a good example of the pros and cons concerning Jews that Englishmen like himself found worth noting.

INFLUENCES ON THE COMPOSITION OF
THE MERCHANT OF VENICE

The following extracts indicate the complex, not to say contradictory, attitudes toward Jews in the early modern period during which Shakespeare grew up and began writing plays. He may not have read any of the documents himself, but he must have been aware of the ideas put forth in them as they were current and debated by intellectuals as well as church officials. They were part of the *Zeitgeist*, the temper of the times, to which every intelligent Elizabethan would have been sensitive. If they do not have a direct influence on the composition of *The Merchant of Venice* they clearly have an indirect influence, and a very powerful one. Luther's tract, for example, may help to explain Antonio's "mercy" to Shylock in requiring his conversion to Christianity. His hope for reconciliation between Christians and Jews anticipates in some ways Shylock's desire to be friends with Antonio and have his love (1.3.134). Descriptive passages (in italics) have been added to clarify the context of this document.

FROM MARTIN LUTHER, "CHRIST WAS BORN A JEW" (1523)
(trans. and ed. Walther I. Brandt, in *Luther's Works*. 55 vols.
Philadelphia, PA: Muhlenberg Press, 1962, 45:199–229)

Martin Luther launched the Protestant Reformation in 1517 with his ninety-five theses nailed to the church door at Wittenburg. His treatise, "Christ Was Born a Jew" (1523), was motivated by the charge he was teaching that "Jesus was conceived of the seed of Joseph, and that Mary was not a virgin, but had many sons after Christ" (Brandt, Introduction, 197). In the first part of his treatise, Luther demonstrates that Jesus was born a Jew, but begotten by a miracle; in the second part, Luther appeals to Christians to be kinder to Jews in the hope of converting them. He ends with arguments demonstrating through scripture and history that Jesus is the true Messiah.

Luther hopes by his arguments to bring the Jews "back to their own true faith [Christianity]." He deplores the ways so-called Christians— "the popes, bishops, sophists [i.e, schoolmen], and monks" have treated Jews so that "anyone who wished to be a good Christian would almost

have had to become a Jew" (p. 200). "If I had been a Jew and had seen
such dolts and blockheads given and teach the Christian faith, I would
sooner have become a hog than a Christian" (p. 200). He continues:

They have dealt with the Jews as if they were dogs rather than human
beings; they have done little else than deride them and seize their property. When they baptize them they show them nothing of Christian doctrine or life, but only subject them to popishness and monkery. When
the Jews then see that Judaism has such strong support in Scripture, and
that Christianity has become a mere babble of without reliance on Scripture, how can they possibly compose themselves and become right good
Christians? I have myself heard from pious baptized Jews that if they had
not in our day heard the gospel they would have remained Jews under
the cloak of Christianity for the rest of their days. For they acknowledge
that they have never yet heard anything about Christ from those who
baptized and taught them. . . . I hope that if one deals in a kindly way
with the Jews and instructs them carefully from Holy Scripture, many of
them will become genuine Christians and turn again to the faith of their
fathers, the prophets and patriarchs. [Brandt's note: Luther invariably
refers to the righteous believers of the Old Testament as Christians.] They
will only be frightened further away from it if their Judaism is so utterly
rejected that nothing is allowed to remain, and they are treated only with
arrogance and scorn. If the apostles, who also were Jews, had dealt with
us Gentiles as we Gentiles deal with the Jews, there would never have
been a Christian among the Gentiles. Since they dealt with us Gentiles
in such a brotherly fashion, we in our turn ought to treat Jews in a brotherly manner in order that we might convert some of them. For even we
ourselves are not yet very far along, not to speak of having arrived. (pp.
200–201)

• • •

When we are inclined to boast of our position we should remember
that we are but Gentiles, while the Jews are of the lineage of Christ. We
are aliens and in-laws; they are blood relatives, cousins, and brothers of
our Lord. Therefore, if one is to boast of flesh and blood, the Jews are
actually nearer to Christ than we are, as St. Paul says in Romans 9[:5].
God has also demonstrated this by his acts, for to no nation among the
Gentiles has he granted so high an honor as he has to the Jews. For from
among the Gentiles there have been raised up no patriarchs, no apostles,
no prophets, indeed, very few genuine Christians either. And although
the gospel has been proclaimed to all the world, yet He committed the
Holy Scriptures, that is, the law and the prophets, to no nation except
the Jews, as Paul says in Romans 3[:2] and Psalm 147[:19–20], "He de-

clares his word to Jacob, his statutes and ordinances to Israel. He has not dealt thus with any other nation; nor revealed his ordinances to them." (p. 201)

At the end, Luther again appeals for Christian charity in dealing with the Jews:

If we really want to help them, we must be guided in our dealings with them not by papal law but by the law of Christian love. We must receive them cordially, and permit them to trade and work with us, that they may have occasion and opportunity to associate with us, hear our Christian teaching, and witness our Christian life. If some of them should prove stiff-necked, what of it? After all, we ourselves are not all good Christians either. (p. 229)

Richard Hooker (1553–1600) was the foremost English Protestant theologian during the Age of Elizabeth. When he was named Master of the Temple by the Archbishop of Canterbury in 1586, he found that he had to defend the Anglican Church against zealous Puritans. In particular, Hooker felt he had to defend the episcopal structure of the English church against the demands for a Calvinist organization as outlined in Calvin's *Institutes*. The final result was the eight books that comprise Hooker's *Laws*, only the first five of which were published in his lifetime. In them he grounds his discussion on the principles of reason, natural law, history, and tradition, which he saw as the basis of Christianity as practiced by the Anglican Church.

The following excerpt shows Hooker's understanding of the Jewish religion and Christianity's debt to it for some of its practices. Note how important he regards the Sabbath, as Jews observe it, and recall that it is by "our holy Sabbath" that Shylock has sworn, however blasphemously, to have "the due and forfeit" of his bond from Antonio (4.1.35–36). Like Hooker, Shakespeare was familiar with many aspects of Jewish history and religious practices. His use of Old Testament names (e.g., Tubal, Jessica) reveals as much, as well as Shylock's reference to biblical stories, such as Jacob's dealings with Laban (1.3.68–87). It is likely that this familiarity influenced his conception of Shylock and his treatment at the hands of Antonio and the other Christians in *The Merchant of Venice*.

FROM RICHARD HOOKER, *OF THE LAWS OF ECCLESIASTICAL POLITY*, Book 5 (1597)
(London, 1594–1600)

Church is a word which art has devised thereby to sever and distinguish that society of which professeth the true religion from the rest which professeth it not. There have been in the world from the very first foundation thereof but three religions: Paganism, which lived in the blindness of corrupt and depraved nature; Judaism, embracing the law which reformed heathenish impiety and taught salvation to be looked for through one whom God in the last days would send and exalt to be Lord of all; finally, Christian belief, which yields obedience to the gospel of Jesus Christ and acknowledges him the Savior whom God did promise. (p. 184)

• • •

If it be then demanded whether we observe these times as being thereunto bound by force of divine law, or else only by positive ordinances of the church, I answer this, that the very law of nature itself, which all men confess to be God's law, requires in general no less the sanctification of times and places, persons and things unto God's honor. For which cause it has pleased him heretofore as of the rest so of time likewise to exact some parts by way of perpetual homage never to be dispensed withal nor remitted again to require some other parts of time with as strict exaction but for less continuance, and of the rest which were left arbitrary to accept what the church shall in due consideration consecrate voluntarily unto like religious uses. Of the first kind amongst the Jews was the Sabbath day; of the second, those feasts which are appointed by the law of Moses; the feast of dedication invented by the church stands in the number of the last kind. The moral law requiring therefore a seventh part throughout the age of the whole world to be that way employed, although with us the day be changed in regard of a new revolution begun by our Savior Christ, yet the same proportion of time continues as which was before, because in reference to the benefit of creation and now much more of renovation thereunto added by him which was Prince of the world to come, we are bound to accompt [count] the sanctification of one day in seven a duty which God's immutable law doth exact forever. The rest they say we ought to abolish, because the continuance of them doth nourish wicked superstition in the minds of men; besides, they are all abused by papists, the enemies of God, yea certain of them as Easter and Pentecost even by the Jews.

Touching Jews, their Easter and Pentecost have with ours as much affinity as Phillip the Apostle with Phillip the Macedonian king. As for "imitation of papists" and "breeding of superstition," they are now become such common guests that no man can think it discourteous to let them go as they came. (pp. 195–96)

• • •

The joy that sets aside labor disperses those things which labor gathers. For gladness does always rise from a kind of fruition and happiness, which happiness banishes the cogitation of all want; it needs nothing but only the bestowing of that it has; in as much as the greatest felicity that felicity has is to spread and enlarge itself, it comes hereby to pass that the first effect of joyfulness is to rest, because it seeks no more; the next, because it abounds, to give. The root of both is the glorious presence of that joy of mind which rises from the manifold considerations of God's unspeakable mercy, into which considerations we are led by occasion of sacred times. For how could the Jewish congregations of old be put in mind by their weekly Sabbaths what the world reaped through his goodness which did of nothing create the world; by their yearly Passover what farewell they took of the land of Egypt; by their Pentecost what ordinances, laws, and statutes their fathers received at the hands of God; by their feast of Tabernacles with what protection they journeyed from place to place through so many fears and hazards during the tedious time of forty years travail in the wilderness; by their annual solemnity of Lots, how near the whole seed of Israel was unto utter extirpation, when it pleased that great God, which guides all things in heaven and earth, so to change the counsels and purposes of men, that the same hand which had signed a decree in the opinion both of them that granted and of them that procured it, irrevocable, for the general massacre of man and woman and child, became the buckler of their preservation that no one hair of their heads might be touched—the same days which had been set for the pouring out of so much innocent blood were made the days of their execution whose malice had continued the plot thereof, and the selfsame persons that should have endured whatsoever violence and rage could offer were employed in the just revenge of cruelty to give unto blood thirsty men the taste of their own cup. (p. 203)

Although not printed until 1561, the play entitled *An Enterlude of the Vertuous and Godly Queene Hester* belongs to an earlier period, probably between 1522 and 1527 and was, in part, an attack upon Cardinal Wolsey, Henry VIII's chancellor, who fell from favor in 1529 (see Walker, 1991 pp. 102–32). The author is unknown, though some attribute the play to John Skelton (1460?–1529), who wrote satirical verse against Wolsey. A morality drama based on the Book of Esther, *Godly Queene Hester* includes allegorical figures of Pride, Adulation, and Ambition along with biblical characters and the clown, Hardydardy. Anachronisms abound, as in Renaissance paintings, to suggest that the incidents of the play are contemporaneous with early sixteenth-century England. For example, when war is mentioned, it is with Scotland or France, not a biblical foe of Persia (Walker 1991, 103). The play remained sufficiently popular to be revived in 1592, when Marlowe's *The Jew of Malta* was also being staged. Unlike Marlowe's play, it shows a much more positive view of Jews, and as such it is a further indication of the dual image of Jews that was current in Shakespeare's England. Recognition of this fact helps to inform our understanding of Shakespeare's portrayal of Shylock, who is neither villain nor hero but a combination of both, just as Jews were regarded as neither devils nor angels but a mixture of both traits. The pleas of the Jews for understanding and mercy anticipate not only Shylock's defense of himself as a human being like everyone else (3.1.50–69), but also his appeal for a means whereby he may continue to support himself after his goods are confiscated (4.1.370–73), although the context in this play is not as ambiguous as it is in *The Merchant of Venice*. Descriptive passages have been added throughout to clarify the context of the document.

FROM *AN ENTERLUDE OF THE VERTUOUS AND GODLY QUEENE
HESTER* (ca. 1522–27)
(Ed. W. W. Greg, from the quatro of 1561. In "Materialen zur
Kunde des alteren Englischen Dramas"; Louvain: A. Uystprust,
1904)

Queen Hester, or Esther, foster child of the Jew Mardochus (Mordechai), is married to King Assuerus (Ahasuerus, or Atarxerxes of Persia), whose chancellor is Aman (Haman). Aman tells the king that the Jews are seditious and conspiring with others to rebel. They must be killed (lines 728–57). Assuerus agrees, and Aman begins to carry out his plan.

After a colloquy between Aman and Hardydardy, a Jew enters and laments:

> O Lord, what a thing is cruelty
> When to it is annexed covetous and pride;
> It destroys both town and country
> Also all regions on every side.
> All is for him too little, his mouth is so wide,
> His rigor ravenous spares not to spill
> Both man and child to have his own will.

This ravenous wolf Aman I do mean,
That hath persuaded the king to kill and slay,
And from all this province to avoid clean
All men and women and children that be
Jews born and of the Jews' consanguinity.
This precept is set up men to remember
And it shall be executed the 13 day of December.
Alas, that ever should fortune such rage
From so cankered a caitiff to proceed;
It is his mind, my head I lay to gage,
All those to slay. I assure you indeed,
That will not by flattery his presumptions feed;
He would be glorified above creatures all,
And yet I trust as Lucifer deep he shall fall.

Another Jew:

The Mantuans thought it a great punishment
To be proscribed from their goods and land,
As reciteth Virgil, that poet eloquent;
Much more is our pain, ye may understand,
That shall lose our lives unless God take in hand
Us to deliver, or else we not can
Avoid the murder of this carnifex [i.e., butcher], Aman.

Another Jew:

He shall by this murder our goods win
And himself enlarge, his pride to advance;
And when he hath all, he shall be new to begin
Ever more to get by some other chance.

Mardochus:

Yet at the last all shall come to mischance;
For both him and his, God shall make tame,
And for their pride and pillage send them worldly shame.

Hester:

Mardochus with your company
We have heard your lamentation,
To our grief and displeasure, verily;
Yet we trust by meek supplication,
First unto God by humble oration
And then to the king by desire cordial
A mean to find for to safeguard ye all.
Call in the chapel [i.e., choir] to the intent they may
Sing some holy hymn to speed us this day.

Then the chapel do sing.

After this prayer and for our former abstinence

To the good Lord I call for comfort
To inspire the prince and his mind incense [i.e., dispose]
That I may obtain now at my resort
To redeem the Jews, all the holy sort,
Also to disclose the false favel [i.e., deceit] and fraud
Of this cruel Aman to thy praise and laud. (813–69)

Hester then goes to the king, invites him with Aman to a banquet, and, first identifying herself with the Jews (915); tells him of Aman's plot to kill them all. She also describes Aman's "pomp and pride" and his lust to obtain everything, so that now his treasure is greater than the king's. (This is an obvious parallel to Wolsey and Henry VIII.) Assuerus says:

He signified unto me that the Jews did
Not feed the poor by hospitality;
Their possessions, he said, were all but hid,
Among themselves lying voluptuously,
Thinking the same might be verily
Much better employed for the common weal
Where now it little profiteth or never a deal.
                    Hester:
    Noble prince, as for hospitality,
Of the Jews dwelling in your region,
It is with them as always hath been
Since the beginning of their possession,
Which God to them gave, of his mere motion [i.e., his own
    initiative],
Also great knowledge of both cattle and grain,
That none of them like household could maintain.
Is not of Abraham the hospitality
In scripture noted and of noble fame
But one honoring when he received three
The Trinity figured in the same?
Both Isaac and Jacob had a like name
Of whom the twelve tribes descended be,
Which ever did maintain hospitality.
    Since God therefore hath begun their household
And aye hath preserved their hospitality,
I advise no man to be so bold,
The same to dissolve whatsoever he be;
Let God alone, for he shall be orderly,
A *fine ad finem*, both here and there,
Omnia disponere suaviter

[From end to end, both here and there,
Disposing everything pleasantly]. (943–70)

Assuerus accepts Hester's plea and dresses down Aman. Aman then pleads for mercy from Hester, who disdains him. Arbona tells Assuerus that there are a couple of gallows in Aman's house he intended to use for Mardochus, but Assuerus decides to hang Aman instead (971–1009). A comic dialogue ensues between Assuerus and Hardydardy in which the "biter bit" theme (in which the evildoer is given a taste of his own medicine) is developed. Arbona comes in and announces Aman's death, intestate, whereupon Assuerus gives his treasure to Hester. Hester then confesses that Mardochus is her father's brother, descended from the stock of Benjamin. Assuerus says this truth was well known to him before and promotes Mardochus, giving him the ring and seal (an allusion perhaps to Henry VIII and Cranmer, whom Henry advanced over his enemies).

Hester begs that the edict against the Jews be revoked. She further asks that his councillors "peruse" the nation, and if any Jews have abused the law of Moses, they should be constrained to observe it. She concludes:

The Jews be the people of God elected,
And wear his badge of circumcision.
The daily prayer of that holy sect—
[Such] as the psalms of David by ghostly inspiration,
Also holy ceremonies of God's provision—
To God is vailable [i.e., serviceable], that nothing greater,
And all the whole realm for them fares the better.

Assuerus grants Hester's petition and recognizes the moral of the tale, that the head of state should not neglect his people to pursue his own pleasures. Hester adds her own homily on those servants who are false but eventually found out and punished: "The higher they climb, the deeper they fall" (1169–75).

The trial and execution of Dr. Roderigo Lopez (1594), a Portuguese Jew who had converted to Christianity and was indicated for conspiracy in a plot to poison Queen Elizabeth, took place in 1594. The most important details of the events concerning the Lopez affair were recorded in the 1594 *Calendar of State Papers, Domestic*. As an "induction," or prelude, the report recounts the grounds of all plots against Queen Elizabeth, especially by the

Pope and King Philip of Spain. When the Spanish Armada, formed to attack and invade England, failed in 1588, Elizabeth's enemies resorted to treachery: "what they could not do by the cannon, they attempt by crowns" (p. 446).

Many plots against Elizabeth were fomented by Jesuits and seminary priests, using needy and desperate men. The most notorious of the suspected malefactors was the Queen's physician, Dr. Lopez (or Lopes), whose indictment aroused a good deal of anti-Semitism as well as feelings against Spain. His execution became a public event that attracted large crowds of Londoners. The notorious affair caused Marlowe's play, *The Jew of Malta*, to be revived, since in it Barabas, a villainous Jew, also poisons his enemies, one of many other crimes of which he is guilty before he meets his own ignoble end. The popularity of Marlowe's play and the currents of feeling that the Lopez affair engendered may have led to Shakespeare's composition of *The Merchant of Venice* and to the kinds of anti-Semitism that Antonio and Graziano, among others, display (see Chapter 1). In his history of Queen Elizabeth's reign, William Camden gives further details of the Lopez affair.

FROM THE TRIAL OF DR. RODERIGO LOPEZ (1594)
(*Calendar of State Papers, Domestic* 28 February 1594, pp. 445–48)

Lopez, a perjured murdering traitor, and Jewish doctor, worse than Judas himself, undertook to poison her [i.e., Queen Elizabeth], which was a plot more wicked, dangerous, and destestable than all the former. He was Her Majesty's sworn servant, graced and advanced with many princely favours, used in special places of credit, permitted often access to her person, and so not suspected, especially by her, who never fears her enemies nor suspects her servants. The bargain was made, and the price agreed upon [50,000 ducats], and the fact only deferred until payment of the money was assured; the letters of credit for his assurance were sent, but before they came into his hands, God most wonderfully and miraculously revealed and prevented it. [Details of the conspiracy involving Andrada, Da Gama, Tinoco, and others follow, including Lopez's confession when confronted by Da Gama.] The Commission was adjourned 14 March.

FROM WILLIAM CAMDEN'S *HISTORY OF THE REIGN OF QUEEN
ELIZABETH* (1607–17, 1625)
(London; in Latin 1625; English, 1630. vol. 4, pp. 58–59)

The Spaniards, suspecting the fidelity of the English in a matter of so
great weight, used the help of Roderigo Lopez, a Jew by religion, the
Queen's domestic physician, and of Stephen Ferrera Gama and Emman-
uel Liosie, Portuguese (for many of that nation crept into England in
those days, as retainers to the exiled Don Antonio); who, being apprehended by means of letters intercepted, were about the end of February
arraigned at Guildhall in London, and charged from their own confes-
sions to have conspired to make away the Queen by poison. Lopez,
having been for a long time a man of noted fidelity, was not so much as
suspected, save that outlandish [i.e., foreign] physicians may by bribes
and corruption be easily induced to become poisoners and traitors, till
he confessed "That he was drawn in by Andrada, a Portuguese, to employ
his best and secret service to the King of Spain; that he had received from
his intimate counselor, Christopher Moro, a rich jewel; that he had divers
times thereupon advertised the Spaniards of such things as he could
come to the knowledge of that at length, upon an agreement to receive
50,000 ducats, he had promised to poison the Queen; and that he had
signified as much to the Count de Fuentes and Ibara, the King's secretary
in the Netherlands." Stephen Ferrera confessed, "That the Count de Fuentes and Ibara, when he had given them his faithful promise to conceal
the design, showed him a letter which Andrada had written in Lopez's
name about making away the Queen; and that he himself was likewise
sent by Fuentes to deal with Ferrera and Lopez for hastening the Queen's
death and to promise money to Lopez himself, and honors and prefer-
ments to his children.

At the bar Lopez spoke not so much, but cried out, "That Ferrera and
Emanuel were made of nothing but fraud and lying; that he intended no
hurt against the Queen, but abhorred the gifts of a tyrant; that he had
presented that jewel to the Queen which was sent him from the Spaniard,
and that he had no other design in what he did but to deceive the Spaniard and wipe [i.e., cheat] him of his money." The rest spoke nothing for
themselves, only throwing the whole blame upon Lopez. They were all
of them condemned and after three months put to death at Tyburn, Lopez affirming that he loved the Queen as well as he loved Jesus Christ,
which coming from a man of the Jewish profession moved no small
laughter in the standers-by.

Francis Bacon's "A True Report," written about March 20, 1593/4, gives a full account of the Lopez affair, possibly intended for publication, but not printed until 1657 in the "Resuscitatio." It is included in *The Works of Sir Francis Bacon*, edited by James Spedding, 8, 274–87, with a prefatory article, "The Conspiracy of Dr. Lopez," written by Spedding, pp. 271–74, explaining the context in Bacon's career and historical events. Abbreviated versions of events appear in G. B. Harrison's *Elizabethan Journal, 1591–1594* under appropriate dates (e.g., 25 Feb. 1594, pp. 288–91, on the arraignment of Dr. Lopez [with a picture of Lopez and da Gama facing p. 290]; 7 June 1594, pp. 303–4, the execution of Lopez, Tinoco, and Ferrara da Gama).

Edgar Samuel in *The Journal of the Jewish Historical Society of England* 30 (1987–88), 52, argues that Camden's explanation of Lopez's speech—that he was Jew and therefore his speech was a dishonest equivocation—is mistaken, though accepted by some historians. The second possible interpretation, that Lopez was a sincere Christian, is also unsatisfactory. The Spanish state papers give no indication that the Spanish had a plot to use Lopez to poison the Queen; moreover, Lopez's intercepted correspondence shows that he was a secret Jew and subscribed to the secret synagogue in Antwerp. Lopez was sincere in what he said, Samuel claims, but his words and their meaning were misunderstood. Lopez more likely said, "I love the Queen as well as I love Our Lord," which Camden as a Christian reasonably understood to mean "I love Jesus Christ," but that is not how Jews, who reject the belief in the divinity of Jesus Christ, would have meant "Our Lord." Samuel gives examples of how Portuguese Jews used the term in that period and says that Lopez was sincere in his statement about loving the Queen, but the ambiguous language of this crypto-Jew made a bad impression on the crowd of watchers and on later historians. Samuel believes, with others, that Lopez was unjustly condemned for treason and was in fact loyal to the Queen, "who had treated him kindly with protection and preferment." (See also Katz 1994, 57–101, for a full discussion of events and their interpretation.)

QUESTIONS FOR WRITTEN AND ORAL DISCUSSION

1. Analyze in detail the character of Shylock. What are his good qualities? What are his bad ones? Does he or does he not fit the "dual image" of the Jew that Renaissance writers inherited from the Middle Ages?

2. Compare Shylock with Tubal, his coreligionist (fellow Jew). Is Tubal a "good" Jew, or does he, too, have contradictory character traits? What is his role in 3.1, the only scene in which he appears? Some interpreters say he taunts Shylock and spurs him on to his revenge against Antonio. Do you agree?

3. Discuss Shylock's criticism in 3.1 and 4.1 of Christian behavior, such as seeking revenge or keeping slaves. Is this criticism justified, that is, by the actions of other characters in the play? Does it expose flaws in the morality Christians practice as opposed to what they preach?

4. Compare Shylock with Christopher Marlowe's Barabas in *The Jew of Malta*. What comic aspects, at least early on in *The Merchant of Venice*, does Shylock reveal? Are they indebted at all to the character of Barabas? Compare Shylock also with Gerontus in Robert Wilson's *Three Ladies of London* (1584).

5. Organize a debate on the question of whether Shylock was more sinned against than sinning. Each side should bring detailed evidence from *The Merchant of Venice* but also from the Judeo-Christian moral context in which the play is set to support its arguments.

6. Discuss the problem of revenge. Is it ever justified, and if so when and how? Is Shylock's revenge against Antonio adequately motivated, or is he just taking out on him a grievance against all Christians for the way they have treated him personally and Jews generally?

7. Why doesn't Portia succeed in making Shylock merciful in 4.1? Is her speech directed not only to him, but also to others present in the scene? Is the mercy that the duke and Antonio show Shylock truly merciful, or another version of revenge?

8. Why do you think Shylock accepts conversion to Christianity? In his place, would you do the same? Give your reasons for either point of view.

9. Ralph Waldo Emerson said, "A foolish consistency is the hobgoblin of little minds." What inconsistencies or contradictions do you find in *The Merchant of Venice*, that is, in the characters or their actions? Do these inconsistencies make nonsense of the play, or do they reflect natural human tendencies? Here you may wish to consult Norman Rabkin's essay, "Meaning and *The Merchant of Venice*" in his book *Shakespeare and the Problem of Meaning* (1981).

10. Analyze the Church's position from the Middle Ages to the Renaissance on what is sometimes called "The Jewish Question." How consistent was it? Can the Church be accused in those times of official anti-Semitism? Do both the Catholic and Protestant points of view reveal a good measure of ambivalence? Explain.

11. What positive aspects of Jews and their religion does Richard Hooker identify in Book 5 of the *Laws of Ecclesiastical Polity?* Does Shakespeare represent any of them in *The Merchant of Venice?* If so, which ones, and how? If not, why do you suppose he does not?

12. What do you think Elizabethans must have found appealing in the old play, *Godly Queene Hester?* What moral lessons would they have found applicable in their own time? Are any of them also involved in *The Merchant of Venice?* Is Shakespeare's play in any sense a morality play, too?

13. Hester's marriage to King Assuerus was an intermarriage that ultimately worked to the advantage of the Jews in the king's realm. Does Jessica's marriage to Lorenzo promise any similar benefits? Or does her conversion to Christianity alienate her altogether from her Jewish origins? What is her attitude to her new religion?

14. Compare the Jews in *Godly Queene Hester* with the Jews in the Renaissance. Did they share the same problems? What were their problems, and what recourse did Renaissance Jews have to solve them? Are the problems the same for Jews in Europe today?

15. Why did the trial of Dr. Roderigo Lopez excite so much interest in Shakespeare's day? In what way do you think *The Merchant of Venice* capitalized on the notorious event, even though it was probably first performed several years later? In what way might the play also be a critique of that event?

SUGGESTED READINGS AND WORKS CITED

Cartwright, Kent. *Theatre and Humanism: English Drama in the Sixteenth Century*. Cambridge: Cambridge University Press, 1999.

Fisch, Harold. *The Dual Image: The Figure of the Jew in English and American Literature*. New York: Ktav Publishing House, 1971.

Katz, David S. "The Jewish Conspirators of Elizabethan England." In *The Jews in the History of England, 1485–1850*. Oxford: Oxford University Press, 1994, 49–106.

Rabkin, Norman. "Meaning and *The Merchant of Venice*." In *Shakespeare and the Problem of Meaning*. Chicago: University of Chicago Press, 1981.

Roth, Cecil. *A History of the Jews in England*. 3d ed. Oxford: Oxford University Press, 1964.

Sinsheimer, Hermann. *Shylock: The History of a Character*. 1947. Reprint, New York: Benjamin Blom, 1968.

Walker, Greg. *The Plays of Persuasion: Drama and Politics in the Court of Henry VIII*. Cambridge: Cambridge University Press, 1991.

4

Classical and Renaissance Concepts of Male Friendship

From ancient times through the Renaissance, friendship between men was regarded as the highest form of social relationship, even surpassing that between man and woman in matrimony. In Plato's *Symposium*, for example, Socrates places male friendship higher on the scale of love than he does marriage between the sexes. Homosexual love did not have the stigma it later came to bear in the Judeo-Christian tradition, but Socrates did not consider that the purest or highest form of love. Stories of the devotion between male friends abound in classical literature and throughout later ages. In the Bible, the devotion between David and Jonathan became proverbial. The willingness of one friend to give his life for another was the true test of friendship.

In *The Merchant of Venice* the friendship between Antonio and Bassanio is tested in precisely this way. While some recent stage productions of the play treat it as a homosexual relationship, at least where Antonio is concerned, Shakespeare only barely suggests that this might be the basis of their friendship, especially when Solanio and Salarino discuss Antonio's parting from Bassanio as he leaves for Belmont (2.8.36–53). Portia seems to recognize the threat their relationship may pose for her marriage to Bassanio, and it may account for her use of the ring plot at the end of the play. Since she also recognizes the depth of her husband's love for his friend, she is willing to defer the consummation of their marriage until the problem of Antonio's forfeiture is resolved (3.2.241–324).

The biblical story of David and Jonathan appears in 1 Sam., beginning in chapters 18.1–15 and 19.1–10, continuing through chapters 20.1–43, 31.2–3, and ending with David's lament for Jonathan (2 Sam. 1.17–26). It concludes with the famous lines: "Woe is me for thee, my brother Jonathan. Very kind hast thou been unto me. Thy love to me was wonderful, passing the love of women. How are the mighty overthrown, and the weapons of war destroyed." Another famous story portrayed the friendship of Damon and Pythias, which Elizabethan playwright Richard Edwards (1523–1566) made into a play that was performed before Queen Elizabeth by the Children of the Queen's Chapel, probably at Christmas, 1564. Damon and Pythias (ca. 1564) may also have been performed at Merton College, Oxford, early in 1568.

The story of Damon and Pythias as Edwards dramatizes it contrasts the devoted friendship of the two Greeks against the false friendship of two Sicilians, Aristippus, a philosopher, and Carisophus, a scheming parasite. When Damon and Phythias visit Syracuse in Sicily, accompanied by Damon's servant, Stephano, Damon makes the mistake of telling Carisophus that he wants to go around and see the city, whereupon Carisophus informs the tryannical ruler, Dionysius, that Damon is a spy. Dionysius arrests Damon and condemns him to death. When Damon asks permission to go home to set his affairs in order, Pythias offers himself as a hostage to guarantee his friend's return within three months. Dionysius agrees, but as the day set for Damon's return arrives, Damon does not appear. Pythias is prepared to sacrifice himself for his friend, when Damon appears, running to turn himself in. The two friends argue about who should die. Dionysius becomes so impressed with their devotion to each other that he experiences a moral conversion and frees both of them on condition that they accept him into their fellowship.

Early in the play, their servant Stephano describes the friendship between Damon and Pythias:

> These two, since at school they fell acquainted,
> In mutual friendship at no time have fainted,
> But loved so kindly and friendly each other,

As though they were brothers by father and mother.
Pythagoras learning these two have embraced,
Which both are in virtue so narrowly laced
That all their whole doings do fall to this issue,
To have no respect but only to virtue:
All one in effect, all one in their going,
All one in their study, all one in their doing.
These gentlemen both, being of one condition,
Both alike of my service have all the fruition.
Pythias is joyful if Damon be pleased,
If Pythias be served, then Damon is eased.
Serve one, serve both: so near, who would win them?
I think they have but one heart between them. (ed. 1571; scene 5,
    lines 240–71)

A CLASSICAL VIEW OF FRIENDSHIP: CICERO

The nature of friendship has inspired many discourses on the subject, from classical times to the present. One of the most famous and highly regarded in the Renaissance, often cited by others, was the Roman orator Cicero's *De Amicitia* (Of Friendship). It was translated by Elizabeth I's godson, Sir John Harington in 1550, but was already very influential. Marcus Tullius Cicero (106–43 B.C.), or Tully as he is also known, was the most famous orator of his time. He was also an important politician and statesman during the period of the Roman republic. He actively opposed Julius Caesar during the Roman civil war, but after it ended, Caesar forgave him and he lived as an honored Roman under the dictatorship. Cicero was not a member of the conspiracy against Caesar, which led to the dictator's assassination, but he did not oppose it, although he and Marc Antony were bitter enemies. After Octavius Caesar conquered Rome, Antony persuaded him to have Cicero executed.

Written in the year 44 B.C., *De Amicitia* takes the form of a dialogue among Gaius Laelius, a renowned Stoic and elegant orator, and his two sons-in-law, Quintus Mucius Scaevola, a distinguished lawyer, and Gaius Fannius Strabo, a historian and tribune of the plebians. The time is 129 B.C., shortly after the death of Scipio Minor, who was Laelius's best friend, and is the occasion of the discourse. The following excerpts include some of the principles of friendship that Cicero advocated and that Renaissance authors admired.

FROM CICERO, *DE AMICITIA* (44 B.C.)
(Trans. Sir John Harington, London, 1550)

They which behave themselves, and do so live that their faith, their honesty, their uprightness and liberality is allowed, and in them neither covetousness, neither treachery, neither rashness is seen to be, and beside this be of great constancy . . . all these like as they be taken for good men, so we think them worthy to be called, who follow nature, the best guide of well living, so far as man's power can lead them. For this methinketh I do spy, that we are so born together as there should be among all men a certain fellowship. And the greater the fellowship should be, the nearer that everyone cometh to another. And therefore citizens be dearer to us than foreigners, and kinsfolk nearer than friendfolk. For toward these Nature herself hath bred a friendliness. But in this there is not surety enough, for in this point friendship passeth kindred, in that kindred may be without good will, but friendship can no wise lack it. For take away good will, and friendship loseth; but cousinage keepeth still his name.

But how great the virtue of friendship is, it may hereof best be understood, that of innumerable companies of mankind, which nature herself hath knit together, it is a thing drawn and brought to such a strait, that friendship is always joined either between two, or else between few. For friendship is nothing else but a perfect agreement with good will and true love in all kind of good things and goodly. And I know not whether any better thing hath been given of God unto men, wisdom excepted, than this same friendship. Some set riches before, some health, others power, and others honor, many also pleasures. But certainly this last is for beasts, and those other uppermore be fading and uncertain, and be not so much within the compass of our wisdom as within the fickleness of fortune. But they which place our chiefest weal in virtue do therein very well; and yet, this same virtue it is which both engendereth and upholdeth friendship. Neither may friendship by any means be without virtue.

. . . What sweeter thing can there be than to have one with whom thou darest so boldly talk all matters, as with thine own self? How should the profit of welfare and prosperity be so great if you had not some which should rejoice so much thereat as yourself? But as for evil plight and adversity, it were hard to bear them without such a one as would bear the same more grievously than yourself. To conclude, all other things that are desired, each one to each man serveth the turn, as riches for use, wealth for worship, honor for praise, pleasure for delight, health to want grief and to do the office of the body. Friendship containeth more things in it. Withersoever you turn, it is at hand. It will be kept out of no place; it is never unreasonable, nor ever troublous. Therefore, neither water, nor fire, nor air, as they say, do we in more places use than this friendship. And now I do not speak of the common or mean sort of friendship, which yet delighteth and profiteth, but of the true and perfect, as theirs was, which being few are soon told. For friendship maketh welfare the goodlier, and evilfare—by sundering and parting of griefs—the lighter.

And where friendship hath in it many and great commodities, yet this exceedeth all the rest, that she forecomforts us with the good hope that is to come. She suffereth men's hearts neither to faint nor yet to fall, but he that beholdeth his friend doth, as it were, behold a certain pattern of himself. Wherefore in friendship the absent be present, the needy never lack, the sick think themselves whole, and—that which is hardest to be spoken—the dead never die. So great honor, remembrance, and desire breedeth in them toward their friends. By reason whereof their deaths be thought happy, and others' lives be much praised. But if you should take out of the world the knot of friendship, neither can there any house, neither any city be able to continue; no, not the tillage of the land can endure. And if this cannot be understood hereby, yet of strife and debate it may well be perceived, how great the power of concord and friendship is. For what house so steady, or what city stands so fast, but through hatred and strife it may be utterly overthrown? Whereupon, how much goodness resteth in friendship it may easily be judged.

THE VIRTUE OF FRIENDSHIP

One of the greatest admirers of Cicero, was Sir Thomas Elyot (1490?–1546). He is best known as one of the early sixteenth-century English humanists associated with the court of Henry VIII. Educated at home, he may or may not have attended Cambridge University, but in any case became very well versed in Greek and Latin. Political philosophy and the theory of education especially interested him, as it did his friends Sir Thomas More and Roger Ascham. His book, *The Governor*, dedicated to Henry VIII, went through seven editions (1531–1580) and became very influential. Borrowing ideas from other Renaissance writers such as Erasmus, Francesco Patrizi, and Pico della Mirandola, Elyot stated that its purpose to instruct those "who will be studious about the public weal" in the qualities and particularly the virtues required for positions of responsibility; hence the book's title.

Among the virtues Elyot discusses is friendship, obviously of great importance to politicians, but also important in all walks of life. Like Cicero, Elyot emphasizes compatibility between two persons, goodness, and generosity as qualities essential to true friendship. They are the features that Portia alludes to when she speaks of the relationship between Antonio and Bassanio, as she understands it, in *The Merchant of Venice* (3.4.11–18)—what she refers to as "an equal yoke of love" between the two men. The play dramatizes various types of friendship, but the one between Antonio and Bassanio is the most important and briefly becomes problematical after Bassanio weds Portia and gives away her ring.

Elyot ends his abstract discussion by offering several concrete examples of great friendships. The first two are taken from classical literature and include short summaries of Orestes and Pylades followed by an account of Damon and Pythias. He then devotes a chapter to Boccaccio's narrative of Titus and Gisippus, which focuses on the conflict between friends when the love for a woman complicates their relationship.

FROM SIR THOMAS ELYOT, *THE GOVERNOR* (1531)
(Book II, chapter 11: "The True Description of Amity, or
Friendship," Fol. 141–45)

I have already treated of benevolence and beneficence generally. But forasmuch as friendship, called in Latin *amicitia*, comprehendeth both those virtues more specially, and in an higher degree, and is now so seldom or strange among mortal men by the tyranny of covetousness or ambition, which having long reigned, and yet do so, that amity may be scarce known or found throughout the world by them that seek for her as diligently, as a maiden would seek for a small silver pin in a great chamber strewed with white rushes, I will therefore borrow so much of the gentle reader, though he be well nigh weary of this long matter, barren of eloquence and pleasant sentence, and declare somewhat by the way, of very and true friendship. Which perchance may be an inducement to good men, to seek for persons like themselves, towards whom they may practice friendship. For as Tully saith: "Nothing is more to be loved, or to be joined together, than similitude of good manners or virtues, wherein be the same or similar studies, the same wills or desires"; in them it happeneth, that one in another as much delighteth as in himself.

Aristotle saith: Friendship is a virtue, or joined with virtue. Which is affirmed by Tully, saying: Friendship cannot be without virtue, and in none but good men only. Who be good men, he afterwards declareth, to be those persons, who do so conduct themselves, and in such wise do live, that their faith, surety, equality, and liberality be sufficiently proved. Neither that in them is any covetousness, wilfulness, or foolhardiness, and that in them is great stability or constancy: them suppose I (as they be taken) to be called good men, who do follow (as much as men may) nature, the chief captain or guard of man's life. Moreover, the same Tully defineth friendship in this manner, saying: "It is no other thing, but a perfect consent of all things appertaining as well to God as to man, with benevolence and charity. And that he knoweth nothing given of God, except sapience, to man more commodious." Which definition is excellent and very true. For in God and every thing that cometh from God, nothing is of greater estimation than love, called in Latin, *amor*, whereof *amicitia* cometh, named in English friendship or amity: the which being taken away from the life of man, no house shall abide standing, no field shall be in culture. And that is lightly perceived, if a man do remember, what cometh of dissention and discord: finally he seemeth to take sun from the world that taketh friendship from man's life.

Since friendship cannot be but in good men, nor may it be without virtue, we may be assured that thereof none evil may proceed or therewith any evil thing may participate. Whereof inasmuch as it may be but in a few persons (good men being in a small number), and also it is rare and seldom, as all virtues be commonly. I will declare, after the opinion of philosophers, and partly by common experience, who among good men be of nature most apt to friendship.

Between all men that be good, [there] cannot always be amity, but is also requireth, that they be of similar or much like manners or study, and specially of manners. For gravity and affability, be every of them laudable qualities. So be severity and placability. Also magnificence and liberality be noble virtues: And yet frugality, which is soberness or moderation in living, is (and that for good cause) of all wise men extolled; yet where these virtues and qualities be separately in sundry persons assembled, may well be perfect concord, but friendship is there seldom or never. For that, which the one for virtue embraceth, the other contemneth, or at the least neglecteth. Wherefore it seemeth, that wherein the one delighteth, it is to the other repugnant unto his nature: And where is any repugnance may be none amity, since friendship is an entire consent of wills and desires. Therefore it is seldom seen, that friendship is between these persons: a man sturdy, of opinion inflexible, and of sour countenance and speech, with him that is tractable, and with reason persuaded, and of sweet countenance and entertainment. Also between him who is elevated in authority and another of a very base estate or degree: yea, and if they be both in an equal dignity, if they be desirous to climb, as they do ascend, so friendship for the more part decayeth. For as Tully saith, in his first book of offices: What thing soever it be, in the which the many cannot excel, or have therein superiority, therein oftentimes is such contention, that it is a thing of all others most difficult to keep among them good or virtuous company; that is as much to say, as to retain among them friendship and amity. And it is oftentimes seen, that divers, who before they came in authority were of good and virtuous conditions, being in their prosperity were utterly changed, and despising their old friends, set all their study and pleasure on their new acquaintance. Wherein men shall perceive to be a wonderful blindness, or (as I might say) a madness, if they note diligently all that I shall hereafter write of friendship.

But now to resort to speak of them in whom friendship is most frequent, and they also thereto be most aptly disposed. Undoubtedly it be specially they who be wise and of nature inclined to beneficence, liberality, and constancy. For by wisdom is marked and substantially discerned the words, acts, and demeanor of all men, between whom happeneth to be any intercourse of familiarity, whereby it is engendered a favor or disposition of love. Beneficence, that is to say, mutually putting to their study and help in necessary affairs, induceth love. They that be liberal, do withold or hide nothing from them, whom they love, whereby love increaseth. And in them that be constant is never mistrust or suspicion, nor any surmise or evil report can withdraw them from their affection. And hereby friendship is made perpetual and stable. But if similitude of study or learning be joined unto the said virtues, friendship much rather happeneth, and the mutual interview and conversation is much more pleasant, specially if the studies have in them any delightful affection or motion. For where they be too serious, or full of contention, friendship is oftentimes assaulted, whereby it is often in peril. Where the study is elegant, and the matter illecebrous [i.e., alluring], that is to say sweet to the reader, the course whereof is rather gentle persuasion and quick reasonings, than over-subtle argument, or litigious controversies: there also it happeneth, that the students do delight in one another, and be without envy or malicious contention.

Now let us try out, what is that friendship that we suppose to be in good men. Verily, it is a blessed and stable connexion of sundry wills making of two persons one, in having and suffering. And therefore a friend is properly named of philosophers, the other I. For that in them is but one mind and one possession: and that, which more is, a man more rejoiceth at his friend's good fortune than at his own.

Orestes and Pylades, being wonderful[ly] [a]like in all features, were taken together and presented unto a tyrant, who deadly hated Orestes. But when he beheld them both and would have slain Orestes only, he could not discern the one from the other. And also Pylades, to deliver his friend, affirmed that he was Orestes. On the other part, Orestes, to save Pylades, denied and said that he was Orestes (as the truth was). Thus a long time together contending, the one to die for the other, at the last so relented the fierce and cruel heart of the tyrant, that wondering at their marvellous friendship, he suffered them freely to depart, without doing them any damage. Pythias and Damon, two Pythagoreans, that is to say, students of Pythagoras's learning, being joined together in perfect friendship: for that one of them was accused of having conspired against Dionysius, King of Sicily, they were both taken and brought to the king, who immediately gave sentence that he that was accused should be put to death. But he desired the king that before he died, he might return home to set his household in order and to distribute his goods. Whereat the king laughing demanded of him scornfully, what pledge he would leave him to come again. At which words his companion stepped forth and said that he would remain there as a pledge for his friend, that in case he came not again at the day appointed, he willingly would lose his head. Which condition the tyrant received. The young man that should have died was suffered to depart home to his house, where he did set all things in order and disposed his goods wisely. The day appointed for his return was come, the time much passed; wherefore the king called for him that was his pledge, who came forth merrily, without any appearance of dread, offering to abide the sentence of the tyrant, and without grudging, to die for the saving the life of his friend. But as the officer of justice had closed his eyes with a kerchief and had drawn his sword to have struck off his head, his fellow came running and crying that the day of his appointment was not yet past: wherefore he desired the minister of justice to loose his fellow and prepare to do execution on him that had given the occasion. Whereat the tyrant, being all abashed, commanded both to be brought to his presence; and when he had enough wondered at their noble hearts and their own constancy in friendship, he offering to them great rewards, desired them to receive him into their company, and so doing them much honor, did set them at liberty.

Undoubtedly that friendship which doth depend either on profit or else in pleasure, if the ability of the person who might be profitable do fail or diminish, or the disposition of the person who should be pleasant do change or fail, the ferventness of the love ceaseth, and then there is no friendship.

Following the chapter on friendship in *The Governor* is the story of Titus and Gisippus, taken from Boccaccio's *Decameron*, Day 8. These two noble and loving friends were so much alike (though one was a Roman and the other an Athenian) that they could not be told apart. Elyot uses the story to illustrate the principles of friendship. For example, he describes the men thus:

> These two young gentlemen, as they seemed to be one in form and personage, so, shortly after acquaintance, the same nature wrought in their hearts such a mutual affection that their wills and appetites daily more and more confederated themselves, that it seemed none other, when their names were declared, but that they had only changed their places, issuing (I might say) out of the one body, and entering into the other.

They ate, studied, and delighted both in one doctrine, and so increasingly became one. When it came time for Gisippus to marry, he found a lovely woman and became betrothed; but when he introduced Sophronia to his friend, Titus fell desperately in love to the point that he almost died. Seeing this, Gisippus surrendered her to his friend and arranged for their secret marriage; whereupon Titus was summoned back to Rome with his bride. But the Athenians were so outraged by events, that they confiscated all of Gisippus's fortune and exiled him. Eventually, forlorn and wasted, he goes to Rome, where Titus fails to recognize him. On the point of suicidal despair, Gisippus falls asleep in a barn, where a murderer also takes refuge and causes Gisippus to be charged with the murder he has himself committed. At his trial, Titus finally recognizes his old friend, protests that Gisippus is not the murderer, and demands to be put to death instead. Hearing the dispute between the two friends that followed (like that between Damon and Pythias), the true murderer experiences a change of heart and comes forth from the crowd and confesses. The two friends are once again united in fellowship, and through Titus's efforts Gisippus has all his goods and honors restored to him in Athens. (On the importance of this story in sixteenth-century England see Hutson [1994, 52–64].)

Edmund Spenser (1552?–1599) was perhaps the most illustrious of Shakespeare's contemporaries among the nondramatic poets. His poem, *The Shepheard's Calendar* (1579), first brought him acclaim, but his greatest work is the unfinished epic romance, *The Faerie Queene*, the first three books of which were published in 1590, and the next three in 1596.

In the late 1570s, Spenser entered the service of the earl of Leicester, through whom he met and formed a close friendship with the poet and essayist, Sir Philip Sidney. Their relationship, as well as his study of the classics, doubtless inspired some of his ideas on friendship, which he developed in his poetry. From *The Faerie Queene*, Book IV, his theory of friendship may be inferred and is analyzed in *Spenser's Theory of Friendship* by Charles G. Smith (1935).

Examination of the various episodes in the Fourth Book of the *Faerie Queene*, according to Smith (1935, 27), reveals Spenser's theory of friendship as the harmonizing and unifying principle in the world of man as it is also in the world of nature. This theory is based on certain ideas that seem to satisfy the conditions required by such a conception. Some of the ideas clearly derive from classical and earlier Renaissance sources, such as those of Cicero and Elyot. Expressed in the simplest terms these ideas are (1) friendship is based on virtue, (2) friendship is based on equality,

(3) friendship is based on similarity, (4) friends have but one soul, (5) a friend is a second self, (6) false friendship cannot last, and (7) friends' goods are common goods.

Smith goes on to show where in Book IV these ideas are found and how widespread they were, even becoming proverbial in much Renaissance literature. He shows, too, how Spenser evidently rejected the seventh principle, as he was in no way socialistically inclined. The first three stanzas of *The Faerie Queene*, Book IV, Canto 9, serve as a kind of prologue to the theme of friendship as Spenser develops it, and indicates quite plainly that the love between friends ("Faithful friendship") is superior to the love between the sexes ("Cupid's flame").

FROM EDMUND SPENSER, *THE FAERIE QUEENE*
(London, 1596)

Book IV, Canto 9

I

Hard is the doubt, and difficult to deem,
When all three kinds of love together meet,
And do disport the heart with power extreme,
Whether shall weigh the balance down; to wit,
The dear affection unto kindred sweet,
Or raging fire of love to womankind,
Or zeal of friends combined with virtues meet.
But of them all, the bond of virtuous mind,
Meseems, the gentle heart should most assured bind.

II

For natural affection soon doth cease,
And quenched is with Cupid's greater flame:
But faithful friendship doth them both suppress,
And with mastering discipline doth tame,
Through thoughts aspiring to eternal fame.
For as the soul doth rule the earthly mass,
And all the service of the body frame,
So love of soul doth love of body pass,
No less than perfect gold surmounts the meanest brass.

III

All which who list by trial to assay,
Shall in this story find approved plain;

In which these squires true friendship more did sway,
Than either care of parents could refrain,
Or love of fairest lady could constrain.
For though Poena were as fair as morn,
Yet did this trusty squire with proud disdain
For his friend's sake her offered favors scorn,
And she herself her sire, of whom she was yborne.

MONTAIGNE AND BACON ON THE MEANING OF FRIENDSHIP

Two of the most famous essayists in the sixteenth and seventeenth centuries were Michel de Montaigne (1533–1592) and Sir Francis Bacon (1561–1626). Shakespeare knew Montaigne's work and was directly or indirectly influenced by his skeptical outlook, especially toward the latter part of the dramatist's career. He probably knew Bacon, who was his close contemporary; but if he read any of his essays, it might have been after the composition of *The Merchant of Venice*, since Bacon's first collection of ten essays was not published until 1597. Friendship being a subject of perennial interest, both Montaigne and Bacon wrote essays on the subject. They further develop the themes discussed by their forebears and contemporaries and provide a larger context for understanding the themes as they appear in *The Merchant of Venice*. Montaigne's essay begins by comparing friendship with matrimony, to the latter's disadvantage, and then focuses on the problems of homosexual relationships. Bacon's essay mainly treats the benefits of friendship, such as intimate communication and understanding.

Michael de Montaigne, the eldest son of wealthy parents, was born in the Dordogne region of France near Bordeaux. His mother's family was of Spanish-Jewish origin and, like his father's, prosperous and important. Montaigne was brought up in the Catholic faith. At first tutored at home, where he became proficient in Latin, Montaigne later attended the Collège de Guyenne in Bordeaux and was its star pupil. From 1554 to 1570 he was a counselor in the Parlement de Bordeaux but found the work, preparing and reporting on cases, tedious and dull. The injustice and inadequacy of the laws troubled him and fed his growing skepticism.

During this period he became friends with Etienne de La Boètie, about whom he writes in his essay "Of Friendship," and whose death he deeply mourned. In 1565 Montaigne married, and though he was a dutiful husband, he evidently did not find the conjugal life fulfilling, as his remarks on marriage indicate. In 1568 his father died, leaving him his title and his estate. Two years later Montaigne resigned from his position in the Bordeaux Parlement and, unable to find suitable employment elsewhere, he retired to his estate at the age of thirty-eight. He eventually began writing a series of essays on subjects as diverse as death, pain, solitude, liars, cannibals, and the custom of wearing clothes.

In 1580, Montaigne's first two books of essays were published in Bordeaux. He later traveled with his brother and some friends to Germany, Switzerland, and Italy and kept an account of his visits in his *Travel Journal*. From Italy he was called back to become mayor of Bordeaux. It was a busy and difficult time, and his service ended during a plague in the city that killed nearly half its inhabitants. He returned to his estate and resumed writing, although he also became involved in national politics as an adviser to Henry of Navarre, later King Henri IV of France. He died in 1592, having published further essays and revising earlier ones, whose influence has spread constantly ever since.

FROM MICHEL DE MONTAIGNE, "OF FRIENDSHIP" (CA. 1580)
(Trans. Donald M. Frame, *The Complete Works of Montaigne*;
Stanford: Stanford University Press, 1957, pp. 135–44)

To compare this brotherly affection [of friendship] with affection for women, even though it is the result of our choice—it cannot be done; nor can we put the love of women in the same category. Its ardor, I confess . . . is more active, more scorching, and more intense. But it is an impetuous and fickle flame, undulating and variable, a fever flame, subject to fits and lulls, that holds us only by one corner. In friendship it is a general and universal warmth, moderate and even, besides, a constant and settled warmth, all gentleness and smoothness, with nothing bitter and stinging about it. What is more, in love there is nothing but a frantic desire for what flees from us:

> Just as a huntsman will pursue a hare
> O'er hill and dale, in weather cold or fair;
> The captured hare is worthless in his sight;
> He only hastens after things in flight.
> —Ariosto

As soon as it enters the boundaries of friendship, that is to harmony of wills, it grows faint and languid. Enjoyment destroys it, as having a fleshly end, subject to satiety. Friendship, on the contrary, is enjoyed according as it is desired; it is bred, nourished, and increased only in enjoyment, since it is spiritual, and the soul grows refined by practice. During the reign of this perfect friendship those fleeting affections once found a place in me, not to speak of my friend, who confesses only too many of them in these verses. Thus these two passions within me came to be known to each other, but to be compared, never; the first keeping its course in proud and lofty flight, and disdainfully watching the other making its way far, far beneath it.

As for marriage, for one thing it is a bargain to which only the entrance is free—its continuance being constrained and forced, depending otherwise than on our will—and a bargain ordinarily made for other ends. For another, there supervene a thousand foreign tangles to unravel, enough to break the thread and trouble of the course of a lively affection; whereas in friendship there are no dealings or business except with itself. Besides, to tell the truth, the ordinary capacity of women is inadequate for that communion and fellowship which is the nurse of this sacred bond; nor does their soul seem firm enough to endure the strain of so tight and durable a knot. And indeed, but for that, if such a relationship, free and voluntary, could be built up, in which not only would the souls have this complete enjoyment, but the bodies would also share in the alliance, so that the entire man would be engaged, it is certain that the resulting friendship would be fuller and more complete. But this sex in no instance has yet succeeded in attaining it, and by the common agreement of the ancient schools is excluded from it.

And that other, licentious Greek love is justly abhorred by our morality. Since it involved, moreover, according to their practice, such a necessary disparity in age and such a difference in the lovers' functions, it did not correspond closely enough with the perfect union and harmony that we require here: "For what is this love of friendship? Why does no one love either an ugly youth, or a handsome old man?" [Cicero.] For even the picture the Academy paints of it will not contradict me, I think, if I say this on the subject: that this first frenzy which the son of Venus inspired in the lover's heart at the sight of the flower of tender youth, in which they allow all the insolent and passionate acts that immoderate ardor can produce, was simply founded on external beauty, the false image of corporeal generation. For it could not be founded on the spirit, the signs of which were still hidden, which was only at its birth and before the age of budding. If this frenzy seized a base heart, the means of his courtship were riches, presents, favor in advancement to dignities, and other such base merchandise, which were generally condemned. If it fell on a nobler heart, the means were also noble: philosophical instruction, precepts to revere religion, obey the laws, die for the good of the country; examples of valor, prudence, justice; the lover studying to make himself acceptable by the grace and beauty of his soul, that of his body being long since faded, and hoping by this mental fellowship to establish a firmer and more lasting pact.

When this courtship attained its effect in due season . . . then there was born in the loved one the desire of spiritual conception through the medium of spiritual beauty. This was the main thing here, and corporeal beauty accidental and secondary; quite the opposite of the lover. For this reason they prefer the loved one, and prove that the gods also prefer him, and strongly rebuke the poet Aeschylus for having, in the love of Achilles and Patroclus, given the lover's part to Achilles, who was in the first beardless bloom of his youth, and the handsomest of all Greeks.

After this general communion was established, the stronger and worthier part of it exercising its function and predominating, they say that there resulted from it fruits very useful personally and to the public; that it constituted the strength of the countries which accepted the practice, and the principal defense of equity and liberty: witness the salutary laws of Harmodius and Aristogeiton. Therefore they call it sacred and divine. And, by their reckoning, only the violence of tyrants and the cowardice of the common people are hostile to it. In short, all that can be said in favor of the Academy is that this was a love ending in friendship; which corresponds pretty well to the Stoic definition of love: "Love is the attempt to form a friendship inspired by beauty" [Cicero].

I return to my description of a more equitable and more equable kind of friendship. "Only those are to be judged true friendships in which the characters have been strengthened and matured by age" [Cicero].

For the rest, what we ordinarily call friends and friendships are nothing but acquaintanceships and familiarities formed by some chance or convenience, by means of which our souls are bound to each other. In the friendship I speak of, our souls mingle and blend with each other so completely that they efface the seam that joined them, and cannot find it again. If you press me to tell you why I loved him, I feel that this cannot be expressed, except by answering: Because it was he, because it was I.

Sir Francis Bacon, later viscount St. Albans, was the son of Sir Nicholas Bacon, lord keeper of the Great Seal in Queen Elizabeth's reign, and Anne Cooke, sister to Lord Burghley, Elizabeth's chief counselor. Taken up by the earl of Essex in 1591, he was not involved in Essex's rebellion several years later, the earl's unsuccessful attempt to depose the queen. After Elizabeth's death in 1603, he rose rapidly in the court of James I, succeeding eventually to the office of Lord Chancellor in 1618. But shortly after being created viscount St. Albans in 1621, he was convicted of bribery and banished from the court and Parliament. His public service ended, he devoted the rest of his life to study and writing, having earlier published such books as *The Advancement of Learning* (1605), *Novum Organum* (1620), and two collections of essays.

FROM SIR FRANCIS BACON, "OF FRIENDSHIP" (1625)
(See Ed. Michael Kiernan, *The Essayes or Counsels, Civill and Moral*; Cambridge, MA: Harvard University Press, 1985, pp. 81–88)

A principal fruit of friendship is the ease and discharge of the fulness of the heart, which passions of all kinds do cause and induce. We know diseases of stoppings and suffocations are the most dangerous in the body, and it is not much otherwise in the mind. You may take sarza [sarsparilla] to open the liver, steel to open the spleen, flower of sulphur for the lungs, castorem for the brain; but no receipt [recipe] openeth the heart but a true friend, to whom you may impart griefs, joys, fears, hopes, suspicions, counsels, and whatsoever lieth upon the heart to oppress it, in a kind of civil shrift or confession. . . . [T]his communicating of a man's self to his friend works to contrary effect, for it redoubleth joys and cutteth griefs in half; for there is no man that imparteth his joys to his friend, but he joyeth the more; and no man that imparteth his griefs to his friend, but he grieveth the less. So that it is, in truth, of operation upon a man's mind of like virtue as the alchemists use to attribute to their stone for the man's body, that it worketh all contrary effects, but still to the good and benefit of nature. But yet, without praying in aid of [advocating for] alchemists, there is a manifest image of this in the ordinary course of nature; for, [as] in bodies union strengtheneth and cherisheth any natural action, and on the other side weakeneth and dulleth any violent impression, even so is it of minds.

The second fruit of friendship is healthful and sovereign for the understanding, as the first is for the affections; for friendship maketh indeed a fair day in the affections from storm and tempests, but it maketh daylight in the understanding out of darkness and confusion of thoughts. Neither is this to be understood only of faithful counsel, which a man receiveth from his friend; but before you come to that, certain it is that whosoever hath his mind fraught with many thoughts, his wits and understanding do clarify and break up in the communicating and discoursing with another: he tosseth his thoughts more easily, he marshalleth them more orderly, he seeth how they look when they are turned into words, finally he waxeth wiser than himself, and that more by an hour's discourse than by a day's meditation. . . . Neither is this second fruit of friendship in opening the understanding restrained only to such friends as are able to give a man counsel (they indeed are best), but even without that a man learneth of himself and bringeth his own thoughts to light and whetteth his wits against a stone, which itself cuts not. In a word, a man were better relate himself to a statue or picture than to suffer his thoughts to pass in smother [i.e., to be smothered].

And now, to make this second fruit of friendship more complete, that other point which lieth more open and falleth within vulgar observation—which is counsel from a friend. Heraclitus saith well in one of his enigmas, "Dry light is ever the best"; and certain it is that the light that a man receiveth by counsel from another is drier and purer than that which cometh from his own understanding and judgment, which is ever infused and drenched in his affections and customs. So as there is as from his own understanding and judgment, which is ever infused and drenched in his affections and customs. So as there is as much difference between the counsel that a friend giveth and that a man giveth himself as there is between the counsel of a friend and of a flatterer; for there is no such flatterer as is a man's self, and there is no such remedy against flattery of a man's self as the liberty of a friend. Counsel is of two sorts, the one concerning manners, the other concerning business: for the first, the best preservative to keep the mind in health is the faithful admonition of a friend. The calling of a man's self to a strict account is a medicine sometimes too piercing and corrosive. Reading good books of morality is a little flat and dead; observing our faults in others is sometimes improper for our case; but the best receipt (best, I say, to work and best to take) is the admonition of a friend. . . .

After these two noble fruits of friendship (peace in the affections and support of the judgment) followeth the last fruit, which is, like the pomegranate, full of many kernels—I mean aid and bearing a part in all actions and occasions. Here, the best way to represent to life the manifold use of friendship is to cast and see how many things there are which a man cannot do himself, and then it will appear that it was a sparing speech of the ancients to say, "that a friend is another of himself," for that a friend is far more than himself. Men have their time and die many times in desire of some things which they principally take to heart: the bestowing of a child, the finishing of a work, or the like. If a man have a true friend, he may rest almost secure that the care of those things will continue after him; so that a man hath, as it were, two lives in his desires. A man hath a body, and that body is confined to a place; but where friendship is, all offices of life are, as it were, granted to him and his deputy; for he may exercise them by his friend. How many things are there which a man cannot with any face or comeliness say or do himself? A man can scarce allege his own merits with modesty, much less extol them. A man cannot sometimes stoop to supplicate or beg, and a number of the like.

But all these things are graceful in a friend's mouth, which are blushing in a man's own. So, again, a man's person hath many proper relations which he cannot put off. A man cannot speak to his son but as a father; to his wife but as a husband; to his enemy but upon terms: whereas a friend may speak as the case requires and not as it sorteth with the person. But to enumerate these things were endless. I have given the rule, where a man cannot fitly play his own part, if he have not a friend, he may quit the stage.

QUESTIONS FOR WRITTEN AND ORAL DISCUSSION

1. The opening scene of *The Merchant of Venice* introduces several male friends. Analyze their relationship to each other and particularly to Antonio. Who is Antonio's closest friend? Why do Solanio and Salarino leave as soon as Bassanio and the others arrive? What kind of friend is Graziano to Antonio? to Bassiano?

2. What qualities does Cicero value most highly in friendship? Does the friendship between Antonio and Bassanio reveal them? If not, which ones are lacking, and how serious is this lack?

3. Following Aristotle and Cicero, Sir Thomas Elyot insists that friendship can only exist where there is virtue, that is, only among good men. Are Antonio and Bassanio virtuous men? What evidence is there in their behavior or what others say about them to indicate that they are or are not? Is virtue the basis of their friendship?

4. Elyot notes that friendship cannot exist between persons of different social classes. Are Antonio and Bassanio of equal social status? Note that Antonio is a merchant while Bassanio is of the lower aristocracy. Do you detect a strain of any kind in their relationship? Is Bassanio just using Antonio, or is there a real bond of affection between them?

5. After Bassanio weds Portia, will his position in society also change and affect his friendship with Antonio? What is the relationship between Portia and Nerissa? Are they friends in the sense that Elyot means? Or does Nerissa's subordinate position (as Portia's waiting-woman) make friendship between them impossible?

6. A friend is described as "another I," that is, another self, whereby two persons are as one. Does the friendship of Antonio and Bassanio fit this description? Does Bassanio and Graziano's? If not, what kind of friendship do they have, and how would you evaluate it?

7. From biblical and classical times, praise is heaped on the willingness of one friend to lay down his life for his friend, as in the stories of David and Jonathan, Damon and Pythias, Orestes and Pylades, Titus and Gisippus. Does Antonio's willingness to sacrifice himself for Bassanio fall into the same category? When he contracts the bond with Shylock, does he believe he is laying down his life for his friend? In the trial scene, is Bassanio sincere in saying that he will give himself up to Shylock before he lets Antonio lose one drop of blood (4.1.110–12)? Discuss.

8. Write an essay on Spenser's theory of friendship as it pertains to *The Merchant of Venice*. How many of the conditions of friendship does the friendship of Antonio and Bassanio fulfill? Which ones are lacking,

and how important do you believe they are? Does Spenser set too high an ideal? Can you think of any friendships that satisfy all his conditions?

9. Classical and Renaissance writers, like Plato and Montaigne, did not think that a relationship between a man and a woman could rise as high as one between a man and another man. What reasons do they offer for this view? Do you agree with it? If not, explain why. Do you think the marriage between Bassanio and Portia, for example, will rise to a higher level than the friendship between Bassanio and Antonio? Give reasons for your views.

10. Montaigne also questions the possibility of true friendship among young persons. Why does he hold this position? Do you agree with it? What kind of friendship, or love, does he say is desirable, and what kind is not? What is the basic problem he describes? Compare Montaigne's views with the theme of fancy that the song in *The Merchant of Venice* expresses (3.2.63–72).

11. Find a copy of Plato's *Symposium* in your library. What ideas on friendship does Plato develop that Renaissance writers adopt? Where does physical attraction enter into love or friendship, and how important is it? Is Bassanio's physical beauty an attraction for Antonio? Is his wooing Portia a cause of Antonio's melancholy in 1.1 and later?

12. Sir Francis Bacon says that a principal benefit of friendship is that it affords you the opportunity to unload or unburden yourself to your friend about anything that fills your heart. Does any such unburdening occur in *The Merchant of Venice* between any of the characters? Does the scene between Portia and Nerissa in 1.2 suggest that, despite their different stations in life, they are friends in this sense?

13. Bacon says that another benefit of friendship is that it helps you to understand yourself better by communicating your thoughts to your friend. Is this what happens between Bassanio and Antonio in 1.1? Is this what Lorenzo tries to do with Jessica in 5.1 when she complains that she is never merry when she hears sweet music? Does he succeed?

14. All of the writers on friendship argue that financial benefit should not be and cannot be the basis of any true friendship. How then does the loan Antonio obtains from Shylock for Bassanio's benefit affect their friendship? Is theirs after all not a true friendship, since Bassanio admits he has borrowed from Antonio before and squandered what he has obtained? Discuss in detail.

15. What kind of friends are Salarino and Solanio? They are sometimes portrayed on the stage as foppish young men with no real depth. Is

this how you see them? How similar are their characters, and Salerio's, or can they be distinguished one from the other? If so, how?

SUGGESTED READINGS AND WORKS CITED

Emerson, R. W. "Friendship." In *The Collected Works of Ralph Waldo Emerson*. Edited by Robert E. Spiller. 5 vols. Cambridge, MA: Belknap Press, 1971, 111–27.

Hutson, Lorna. *The Usurer's Daughter: Male Friendship and Fictions of Women in Sixteenth-Century England*. London: Routledge, 1994.

Kahn, Coppélia. "The Cuckoo's Nest: Male Friendship and Cuckoldry in *The Merchant of Venice*." In *Shakespeare's "Rough Magic,"* edited by Peter Erickson and Coppélia Kahn, 104–112. Newark: University of Delaware Press, 1985.

Patterson, Steve. "The Bankruptcy of Homerotic Amity in Shakespeare's *Merchant of Venice*." *Shakespeare Quarterly* 50 (spring 1999): 9–32.

Plato. *The Symposium*. Translated by W. Hamilton. Harmondsworth: Penguin Books, 1951.

Smith, Charles G. *Spenser's Theory of Friendship*. Baltimore, MD: Johns Hopkins Press, 1935.

5

Elizabethan Marriage

The position of women in Renaissance England was quite different from their position today. Women had few rights. For example, they could not attend university, they could not vote or be elected to political office, and they had very limited control over their own property. As children, they were utterly subjugated to their parents, especially their fathers. As wives, they were under the domination of their husbands, who had control of all their personal property. Women had little recourse to the law, which of course admitted no women as judges or attorneys. That is why Portia, capable and intelligent though she maybe, must assume the disguise of Dr. Balthasar in *The Merchant of Venice* when she appears in the trial scene. To enter a man's world, as she and Nerissa do in act 4, they must appear as men. At first, like Rosalind in *As You Like It*, they joke about it (3.4.60–80), but during the trial they behave generally very seriously indeed.

The ideal woman in the sixteenth and seventeenth centuries was one who, at least in men's minds, was submissive, meek, obedient to her lord and master, virtuous, soft-spoken or (better) silent, and modest in both dress and comportment. Were she otherwise, for example, if she dared to oppose her husband's will, she was subject to his discipline, which could involve a beating, or possibly worse. Petruchio's treatment of his shrewish wife, Katherine, in *The*

Taming of the Shrew after they are married would not be considered extraordinary, and certainly not illegal.

Patriarchy was thus the order of the day. Men ran the family, the church, business and trade, the courts, and every other major social enterprise. Women, after all, were the weaker sex, weaker in every sense—intellectually, emotionally, and physically (compare Hamlet's phrase, "Frailty, thy name is woman," 1.2.146). It was only proper, therefore, that women should be subordinated to men. Women were relegated to housekeeping (again, under male supervision) and the breeding of children. The concept of patriarchy, moreover, derives from Scripture, where, according to Gen. 2.18, woman was created as "a help meet" for man. The patriarchs, Abraham, Isaac, and Jacob, later ruled as head of the family and founded the lineage of the children of Israel. But patriarchal structures were and are not limited to the Judeo-Christian tradition. They exist in many other cultures, such as the Taliban in Afghanistan, the Chinese and Japanese in Asia, and in many African cultures, where again women are regarded as less capable than men. Only recently have women fought for and won more rights than they ever had before, at least in the West, although the movement is gradually spreading throughout the rest of the world.

In Shakespeare's England patriarchal control began at birth, where children were concerned. Fathers had complete charge of their offspring and could do with them what they wished. Parental consent was required for marriage. A father could bestow his child in marriage as he saw fit, and the child had little or no recourse, although his or her agreement was advisable, if not required, to forestall rebelliousness or unhappiness. In *Romeo and Juliet*, for example, Juliet's father, Old Capulet, advises her suitor Paris to win Juliet's heart first before he gives his consent to the marriage (1.2.14), but later he orders Juliet to marry Paris, regardless of her feelings (4.5.137–95). Elopements, available to both male and female children, provided one escape from parental tyranny, but they were rare and hazardous.

Unlike Romeo and Juliet, who were in any case of the wealthy aristocracy, young people in sixteenth-century England tended to marry late: the national average for women was between twenty-two and twenty-five; for men, twenty-four to thirty. People married late because they needed to have the economic resources to maintain a family before marrying. The Fool in *King Lear* comments on the dangers of reckless, early marriage:

> The codpiece that will house,
>   Before the head has any,
> The head and he shall louse,
>   So beggars marry many. (3.2.25–28)

Overhasty marriages could and often did lead to poverty for impetuous couples.

The average age for women in the upper levels of society entering their first marriages was lower, however, than that of other women. Hence, fathers took whatever precautions they could to insure that their daughters did not marry unwisely, that is, to a fortune hunter or other undesirable man. If the daughter was still unmarried at the time of her father's death, his will sometimes carried provisions to restrict her freedom of choice or run the risk disinheritance. The conditions in the will of Portia's father are extraordinary—for example, that her husband must choose the right casket—and probably not enforceable legally, but they are a dramatic device to show her father's care for his daughter, that is, his concern that she not choose her mate unwisely. Although Portia in 1.2 bridles against those conditions, she ultimately recognizes their significance and determines to abide by them, even after she finds Bassanio, the person she truly loves.

In Elizabethan England, church weddings were not required for a binding marriage, although of course the Church did its utmost to insist on its role in blessing all unions between men and women. Ecclesiastically as well as legally, all that was required for a marriage to be binding was for the couple to make their vows to each other before witnesses. Notwithstanding, in *The Merchant of Venice*, before sending Bassanio off to Venice to try to rescue Antonio, Portia demands that they first go to church and get married (3.2.301). Once a couple wed and the marriage was consummated, they were bound to each other forever. Divorce was difficult if not impossible, certainly among all but the aristocracy, and then only for the reason of adultery.

Intermarriage between faiths was severely frowned upon; in fact, it was forbidden, unless the non-Christian member of the couple converted. Preachers cited Scripture to this effect, both from the Old and the New Testament. In this respect, the marginal gloss—the annotations in the margin—found in the Geneva Bible beside Gen. 24.3–4 is instructive. There Abraham commands his eldest servant to get a wife for his son Isaac not from among the daughters of the Canaanites but from his own country. The annotation reads: "He would not that his son should marry out of the godly family." A further gloss on verse 37 says: "For the Canaanites were accursed and therefore the godly could not join with them in marriage."

For Christians, Jews fell into the category of the ungodly, or infidels (despite her conversion, Graziano still refers to Jessica as an "infidel" when she arrives at Belmont with Lorenzo, 3.2.216). But in the New Testament allowance was made for some intermarriages. In 1 Cor. 7.14, for example, Paul says: "For the unbelieving husband is sanctified by the wife, and the unbelieving wife is sanctified by the husband." The Geneva Bible glosses: "Meaning, that the faith of the believer hath more power to sanctify marriage than the wickedness of the other to pollute it." Nevertheless, in 2 Cor. 6.14, Paul warns against intermarriage: "Be not unequally yoked with infidels; for what fellowship hath righteousness with unrighteousness?" Although Jessica believes she is "saved" by her husband, who has made her a Christian, Lancelot Gobbo continues to tease her unmercifully on her intermarriage with Lorenzo (3.5.1–23).

After marriage, a wife's possessions reverted to her husband's control, as Portia recognizes when Bassanio chooses the lead casket and thereby wins the right to make her his wife. Since she is in love with him, she does not demur; on the contrary, Portia says she wishes she were "A thousand times more fair, ten thousand times more rich" for his benefit (3.2.154). "Myself, and what is mine, to you and yours / Is now converted," she says:

> But now I was the lord
> Of this fair mansion, master of my servants,
> Queen o'er myself; and even now, but now,
> This house, these servants, and this same myself
> Are yours, my lord's. (3.2.167–71)

While this may sound strange to modern ears, indeed, offensive even to those who are not feminists, to an Elizabethan it did not. Morally as well as legally it was regarded as only right and proper, as many Christian preachers taught and sermonized. A treatise published in London in 1632 called *The Law's Resolution of Women's Rights: or, the Law's Provision for Women: A Methodical Collection of such Statutes and Customes, with the Cases, Opinions, Arguments and Points of Learning in the Law, as Do Properly Concern Women*, makes the point quite clearly in Book III, Section VIII: "That which the Husband hath is his own":

> But the prerogative of the Husband is best discerned in his dominion over all eterne things in which the wife by combination divesteth herself of property in some sort and casteth it upon her governor, for her practice everywhere agree with the theorick of law, and forcing necessity submits women to the affection thereof. Whatsoever the husband had before the coverture either in goods or lands, it is absolutely his own, the wife hath therein no seisin [i.e., right of possession] at all.

The foundation for these views lay, again, in Scripture, in Adam's lordship over Eve and the later patriarchs' rule over their families. At the macro/micro level, as the king was the supreme head of the state, the husband was supreme head of the family. The Protestant Reformation did nothing to change this; instead, it repeatedly stressed wives' subordination to the husbands. It would be centuries before this arrangement changed, although in many practical affairs women in fact did exercise a good deal of control in their families and, when taken by their husbands into business, in commercial enterprises as well.

MARRIAGE AND MORALITY

The following excerpts show how seriously marriage was regarded in the sixteenth century, at least among clergy and others trying to improve morality in society. Shakespeare himself, like his great contemporary Edmund Spenser, apparently believed in married love. In his plays, illicit love ends disastrously, as in *Troilus and Cressida*. Whether or not Shakespeare himself was the victim of a "shotgun marriage," his plays seem to emphasize the need for restraint before marriage, as in *The Tempest*, where Prospero warns his daughter and her fiancé Ferdinand not to engage in any premarital sex (at the end they are discovered together, chastely playing chess). In *The Merchant of Venice* all the couples are interested only in marriage. The one exception is the servingman, Lancelot Gobbo, whom Lorenzo criticizes for seducing a Moorish woman (3.5.35–36).

The first excerpt is from Heinrich Bullinger's treatise on marriage. Bullinger (1504–1575) was a Swiss Protestant reformer and a leader of the Reform Church in Zurich after the death of Huldrych Zwingli (1484–1521), who had led the Reformation in Switzerland. In 1549, he and Calvin compiled the Consensus Tigurnus, and later incorporated his views in the Helvetic Confession (1566), which became the most generally accepted creed in Protestant churches throughout many parts of Europe, including Scotland. Miles Coverdale (1488–1569), educated at Cambridge, was one of the translators of the Bible into English, and an ardent Protestant. He lived abroad for part of his life, especially during the reign of Queen Mary (1553–1558), but returned under Elizabeth I and became well known for his sermons and addresses. He translated Bullinger's tractate on marriage into English.

Bullinger's views on marriage are typically Elizabethan. He argues for the sanctity of marriage, the importance of children's obedience to their parents, and the supremacy of the husband and father. He warns against the dangers of intermarriage, though he recognizes ways in which such marriages may be allowed and can work, provided that the non-Christian spouse follows the religion and teachings of Christianity, as Jessica seems willing to do in *The Merchant of Venice*.

FROM HEINRICH BULLINGER, *THE CHRISTIAN STATE OF MATRIMONY* (1541)
(See Trans. Miles Coverdale; Norwood, NJ: Theatrum Orbis Terrarum, 1974)

CHAPTER 1: THE KNOT AND COVENANT OF MARRIAGE

[A] man [shall] leave his father and mother and cleave unto his wife, and they two shall be into one flesh. These words doth Adam (or else Moses) speak yet out of the mouth of God and thereby declareth the duty knot and covenant of married folks; namely, that the highest love, bond, and unity among them should be this: that no man separate them asunder but only death. This declareth he with two special points. First, there is no man (next unto God) dearer unto us by all reason than is our father and mother. But when they will make discord between married folks, God commandeth a man in that behalf to forsake father and mother and to keep him to his wife. The love therefore in marriage ought to be (next unto God) above all loves.

The second: They two saith he shall be into one flesh, that is to say, one body. Now like as the greatest love—the most excellent and unpainful service, diligence, and earnest labor—is in the parts of a man's body, one doing for another, one loving, defending, helping, and forbearing another, suffering also like joy and like pain one with another; even so ought it to be between man and woman in wedlock. And like as the parts of a man's body separate themselves not one from another afore death, even so must wedlock be a knot unloosable. And like as the parts of a man's body, when they are sundered one from another, conceive an exceeding great anguish and dolor and pain, even so ought it to be an exceeding grief for married folks to be separated.

And thus Moses . . . declareth the first original of holy wedlock layeth also the foundation of laws matrimonial, out of the which all other statutes are taken. . . .

CHAPTER 4: THE RIGHT COUPLING TOGETHER OF CHRISTIAN FOLKS IN MARRIAGE

[T]he Lord saith (Deut. 7.3), "Your daughters shall ye not give to their sons (meaning the unfaithful and infidels), and their daughters shall ye not take for your sons." Therefore, in going about marriage, a Christian man must first look that in handfasting himself to a woman, he make no divorce of the true faith or bring it into peril. For it followeth in the law: "For they shall make your sons to fall away from me and to serve strange gods." And then shall the indignation of the Lord wax hot over you and destroy you shortly. Nevertheless, if there be no danger of falling away from God's truth or of hurting the same, then (concerning marriage) it maketh no matter though the party dwell among infidels or come of unfaithful fathers and mothers. For Boaz, which was grandfather to Jesse, David's father, married a Canaanite of Jericho, even Ruth, whom the Evangelist reciteth in the genealogy of Christ Jesu (Matt. 1). For he was right faithful and abhored all idolatry. . . .

Marriage is a common participation of mind, body, and goods. Now saith Paul, "What unity can a faithful believer have with an infidel? The unbeliever cleaveth to unrighteousness, to darkness, to hypocrisy, to error, even unto the devil and idolatry." Again: The faithful believer despiseth, abhoreth, and condemneth all such things; loveth righteousness and truth of the Gospel, the light, even the Lord, and hath God living in him. How will these two now draw in one yoke? To draw one yoke is a manner of speaking, and is as much to say as to have fellowship and to yoke themselves together in wedlock. To bear a strange yoke is it to take an unfaithful mate, or one to give over himself unto such things as may alienate his mind from God and His truth. And verily, what woman soever taketh an unbelieving man must draw after him in unbelieving and do, see, and hear that which is clean contrary unto faith and hurtful to her soul. The child also shall be brought up in infidelity. And though it come not to pass while the parents be alive, yet happeneth it after the death of the faithful. While such yoked folks also are alive, there is no tranquillity. And finally, the believer must be in continual discord with the unbeliever, or else must he grant unto her and so do against God, against his own soul, and against his conscience. Therefore must we take good advisement beforehand, lest we yoke ourselves, our friends, or our children with unfaithful people to the great hurt of ourselves and ours. . . .

CHAPTER 5: TO A RIGHT MARRIAGE MUST CHILDREN ALSO HAVE THE CONSENT OF THEIR PARENTS

Moreover, like as God and faith should not be denied or forsaken with the marriage, even so they which are next unto God (as father and mother) ought not to be neglected and despised. For though God said, "A man shall forsake father and mother and keep him to his wife," yet those His words in that same place are concerning marriage that is made already (what duty they that are married owe one to the other) and are not touching the contracting of wedlock, that children may marry without the respect, knowledge, or consent of their parents, under whose authority and jurisdiction they be. . . . Whereas laws both natural (divine specially) and civil require the parents' consent to the childrens' marriage, in so much that they judge the promise to be of no value which is made without the knowledge of the parents; yea, and that also in those children which are not yet come to their years and are yet under the tuition of their elders. For inasmuch as the children are not yet come to perfect discretion, they cannot contract marriage which requireth understanding; yea, they can neither counsel nor help themselves. So in this behalf the consent of their parents is not only necessary, but also good and profitable for them.

As for privy contracts which are not made according to the laws, they have ever been rejected, neither were they acceptable to any man, save unto such as were ignorant or wicked. For why? For the most part they are made of some fond [i.e., foolish] affection; yea, knavery, falsehood, and deceit is commonly the doer to persuade and by words to take young folks in the snare. Many privy contracts are brought to pass with flattery, with drunkenness, with rewards and promises whereby young, ignorant people are utterly beguiled and destroyed. To give liberty and license unto such is even as much as to give a madman a sword, or a knife to a young child; yea, very slandering is it and a dishonoring of marriage.

Disobedience of children also toward their parents and tutors hath ever been reprehended among all nations. God commandeth and saith, "Thou shalt honor thy father and thy mother" (Exod. 20). Now both the obedience or disobedience of the children at no time declare itself more than in contracting of wedlock. Greater honor canst thou not show unto thy parents than when thou followest them herein; neither greater dishonor canst thou not show unto thy parents than when thou herein resisteth them. Esau displeased his parents very sore in taking a wife without their consent. Jacob followed their mind and was commended. This commandment also of honoring our parents did our Lord Christ right faithfully commit unto us (Matt. 4).

Edwin Sandys, or Sandes (1516?–1588), was persecuted for his Protestant views under Queen Mary in 1555. In 1532, Sandys went to Cambridge, noted for its Reformation principles, where his religious views were, if not implanted, then confirmed. There he became friends with Martin Bucer (1491–1551), the Protestant theologian. In 1553, Sandys was vice-chancellor of the university when Edward VI died and his sister, Mary, acceded to the throne and attempted to reverse the English Reformation; whereupon Sandys resigned his vice-chancellorship and was imprisoned in the Tower of London. He later managed to flee to the Continent until Mary died and Elizabeth succeeded her. Returning to England, he was made Bishop of Worcester in 1559 and in 1570 Bishop of London.

In 1575–1576, his puritan views notwithstanding, he rose to the archibishopric of York, the second highest ecclesicastical office in the Church of England.

Like Bullinger and others, Sandys argues for the supremacy of the husband in marriage and the wife's dutiful subservience to him. He also recognizes the importance of a husband's duties to his wife and generally the responsibilities of both partners in marriage. He especially warns against the attractions of beauty and wealth in choosing a spouse, and insists that marriage be approved by the couple's parents or guardians. Such emphasis on parental guidance may underlie Portia's obedience to the requirements in her father's will, in contrast to Jessica's decision to elope with Lorenzo.

FROM EDWIN SANDYS, *SERMONS*
(London, 1585)

Sermon Sixteen, Preached at a Marriage in Strausborough
[Strasbourg]

DUTIES OF HONOUR REQUIRED IN THE WIFE

Touching the duties of honour which the wife doth owe to the husband, we find in the beginning of the book of Genesis that because of her transgression (for Eve seduced Adam, not Adam Eve) God gave her a law of subjection to her husband, that she might ever after be better directed by him, than he had at that time by her. (Gen. 3.16) . . . St. Paul also, in his Epistle to the Ephesians and Colossians, putteth wives in remembrance of this subjection: "Wives, submit to your own husbands, as to the Lord: because the man is the head of the wife, as Christ is the head of the church. And therefore, as the church is in subjection to Christ, so ought wives to be in subjection to their husbands" (Eph. 5.22–24). What should we seek more reasons? This one is sufficient. God hath set the husband over the wife in authority, and therefore she ought willingly and dutifully to obey him; else she disobeyeth that God, who created woman for man's sake and hath appointed man to be woman's governor. . . .

Yea, we are taught that wives should be of so good behavior and of such modest conversation that by their chaste and mild life and the sweetness of their godly manners they might win their evil husbands unto God, and of atheists make Christians. St. Paul in his Epistle to Titus also teacheth a wife her duty; that is, that she "go appareled as becometh holiness; that she be no quarreler or false acuser, but study to be sober, to love her husband, to love her children, to be discreet, chaste, abiding at home, good and obedient to her husband" (Tit. 2.3–5). "Obey in all things," saith Paul, "even as it becometh you in the Lord" (Col. 3.18). So that, except it be against God's word, the wife ought in all things to obey her husband. . . .

An honest and a modest woman is an honor to her husband; but the dissolute wife and undiscreet is a death. She may not be a gadder abroad, a tatler, or a busy-body, but sober, quiet, and demure; not an open teacher but ready to learn of her husband at home; obedient in all lawful things; taking example of Sarah and giving example to the younger women of well demeaning themselves. Thus the man and wife joining themselves together in true love, endeavoring to live in the fear of God, and dutifully behaving themselves one towards the other, either of them bearing wisely the other's infirmities, doubtless they shall reap joy and comfort by their marriage: they shall find this their estate, which "is honorable in all," happy and profitable unto them. (pp. 319–21)

THE CAUSE OF IRRELIGIOUS MARRIAGE: THE OVER-GREAT RESPECTING OF BEAUTY OR WEALTH

But the common sort of men . . . have chiefly two outward untoward respects, regarding nothing in their choice except it be either beauty or money. The sons of God of old, bewitched with the beauty of the daughters of men, procured the general flood to overflow them all and to wash the defiled world. Sampson took one of the daughters of the Philistines to wife, because she pleased his eye, but what came of it? It cost him a polling [i.e., haircut], wherein stood his strength; and it lost him both his eyes, which before were ravished in the beauty of that deceitful woman. Others there are yet of a baser note, whose only care is to match themselves wealthily. Their question is with what money, not with what honesty, the parties whom they seek are endowed; whether they be rich, not whether they be godly; what lands they have on earth, not what possessions are laid up in heaven for them. Such as marry for money, as the money wasteth, so their love weareth; neither is there any love or friendship constant, save only that which is grounded in constant causes, as virtue and godliness, whereof neither time nor man can spoil us. . . . In marriage therefore it behooveth us to be careful, that they whom we choose be of the household of God, professing one true religion with us; the disparagement wherein is the cause of all dissension, true friendship being a loving consent, as in all things, so chiefly in God's true service. (pp. 324–25)

MARRIAGE WITHOUT CONSENT OF PARENTS

But this is not enough. For although the parties married be such as the law of the Lord alloweth to come together, yet can it not be said that they marry in the Lord, except they also marry in such sort as the law prescribeth. For marriage may be as much dishonored by the one as by the other. For orderly entering into the state of matrimony, it is required that they, which be under the tuition and government of others, have the full consent of their parents, tutors, or such as have rule over them, to direct and guide them. Abraham provided a wife for his son Isaac; Isaac sent Jacob into Mesopotamia to his uncle Laban and there commanded him to take a wife, and he did so (Gen. 24.2–4, 28.1–2). In the law of Moses children are commanded to honor their parents (Exod. 20.12). And what honor is given unto parents if in this chief case, being the weightiest one of them that can happen in all their life, their advice, wisdom, authority, and commandment be condemned? . . . If promises made to God without consent of parents are of no effect, can promises made to men be effectual where parents' consent is not had? "Children," saith the apostle, "obey your parents in all things" (Col. 3.20). In all things, and not in the greatest of all? . . . And as the parents' or tutors' consent is to be had in all good and lawful marriages, so it is against the duty of good parents, either to keep their children longer unmarried than is convenient, or through an over-great desire of enriching them (which is the common disease) to marry them against their liking. Such marriages seldom or never prove well but are for the most part the cause of great sin and much misery. There can be no lawful and commendable match where there wanteth full consent and agreement of the parties whom it most concerneth. Rebecca was asked whether she would go with Abraham's servant and be married unto Isaac, or no (Gen. 24.58). Her parents did neither keep her back from marriage when she was fir for it, nor conclude it till her own mind were known. Such then as marry not in the fear of God, making a religious and a godly choice, having the full consent of their parents or tutors: it is not he that coupleth and joineth them together: their estate is base and not honorable in his sight. (pp. 325–27)

Though Henry Smith (1550?–1591) was heir apparent to a large patrimony, he opted instead to enter the ministry. He did not undertake a pastoral duty, preferring (for conscientious scruples) a lectureship instead. Thomas Nash in his *Piers Penniless* (1592) refers to him as a poet, although none of his poetry is now known. In the 1580s Smith preached in and around London with great success. He became known as "silver-tongued Smith" and was regarded as the prime preacher of the nation, especially for his fluent, eloquent, and practical way of speaking. Although puritanically inclined, Smith was in sympathy with the Church of England. His sermons are notable examples of English prose and pulpit oratory. They are free to an amazing extent of the inveterate vices of his age: vulgarity, quaintness, and affected learning.

Smith's *A Preparative to Marriage* is like a textbook for matrimony, comparable to other such books published in the late sixteenth century, such as William Perkins's *Christian Oeconomy* (ca. 1594) (not excerpted here). Smith carefully gives the chief reasons for getting married: propagation of the species, the avoidance of fornication, and the need for companionship. He gives five criteria in the choice of a good wife, the most important of which is her "fitness and godliness." It may surprise us that a woman's silence is also essential, although this quality can hardly apply to many of Shakespeare's comic heroines, and certainly not to Portia, who can be and is quite voluble. Smith warns against resisting parental guidance in choosing a spouse and against intermarriage, which includes marrying Jews or (perhaps chiefly in sixteenth-century England) Protestants marrying Roman Catholics. Smith also has many positive things to say about the nature of marriage and the responsibilities of both husband and wife. He emphasizes the "community" between husband and wife, which Portia recognizes when she asks Bassanio to share with her the bad news that arrives from Venice (3.2.241–48).

FROM HENRY SMITH, *A PREPARATIVE TO MARRIAGE*
(London, 1591)

THE THREE CAUSES OF MARRIAGE

Now it must needs be, that marriage, which was ordained of such an excellent Author, and in such a happy place, and of such an ancient time, and after such a notable order, must likewise have special causes for the ordinance of it. Therefore, the Holy Ghost doth show us three causes of this union. One is, the propagation of children, signified in that when Moses saith, "He created them male and female" (Gen. 1.27), not both male, nor both female, but one male and the other female, as if he created them to propagate other. And therefore when he had created them so, to show that propagation of children is one end of marriage, he said unto them, "Increase and multiply" (Gen. 1.28), that is, bring forth children, as other creatures bring forth their kind. For this cause marriage is called *matrimony*, which signifieth mothers, which were virgins before. . . . If children be such a chief end of marriage, then it seems that where there can be no hope of children, for age or other causes, there marriage is not so lawful, because it is maimed of one of its ends and seems rather to be sought for wealth or for lust than for this blessing of children. It is not good grafting of an old head upon young shoulders, for they will never bear it willingly but grudgingly. (p. 13)

• • •

The second cause is to avoid fornication. This Paul signifieth when he saith: "For the avoiding of fornication, let every man have his own wife" (1 Cor. 7.2). He saith not for avoiding of adultery, but for avoiding of fornication, showing that fornication is unlawful, too, which the papists make lawful in maintaining their stews, as a stage for fornicators to play upon and a sanctuary to defend them. (p. 15)

• • •

The third cause is to avoid the inconvenience of solitariness, signified in these words, "It is not good for man to be alone" (Gen. 2), as though he had said, this life would be miserable and irksome and unpleasant to man if the Lord had not given him a wife to company his troubles. If it be not good for man to be alone, then it is good for man to have a fellow. . . . Therefore, for mutual society God coupled two together, that the infinite troubles which lie upon us in this world might be eased with the comfort and help one of another, and that the poor in the world might have some comfort as well as the rich. . . .

FIVE RULES IN THE CHOICE OF A GOOD WIFE

There be certain signs of this fitness and godliness, both in the man and the woman. If thou wilt know a godly man, or a godly woman, thou must mark five things: the report, the looks, the speech, the apparel, and the companions, which are like the pulses that show whether we be well or ill. The report, because as the market goeth, so they say the market men talk. A good man commonly hath a good name, because a good name is one of the blessings which God promiseth to good men, but a good name is not to be praised from the wicked. And therefore Christ saith, "Cursed are you when all men speak well of you" (Luke 6.26); that is, when evil men speak well of you, because this is a sign that you are of the world, "for the world liketh and praiseth her own" (John 15.19). . . .

The next sign is the look, for Solomon saith, "Wisdom is in the face of a man" (Eccles. 8.7); so godliness is in the face of a man, and so folly is in the face of a man, and so wickedness is in the face of a man. And therefore it is said in Isaiah 3.9, "The trial of their countenance testifieth against them," as though their looks could speak. One saith well, a modest man dwells at the sign of a modest countenance, and an honest woman dwelleth at the sign of an honest face, which is like the gate of the temple that was called beautiful (Acts 3.2), showing that if the entry be so beautiful, within is great beauty. . . .

The third sign is her speech, or rather her silence; for the ornament of a woman is silence. And therefore the law was given to the man rather than to the woman, to show that he should be the teacher and she the hearer. As the echo answereth but one word for many which are spoken to her, so a maid's answer should be a word, as though she sold her breath. The eye and the speech are the mind's glasses [i.e., mirrors]; "for out of the abundance of the heart," saith Christ (Matt. 12.34–36), "the mouth speaketh"; as though by the speech we might know what aboundeth in the heart. And therefore he saith, "By thy words thou shalt be condemned." That is, thou shalt be justified to be wise, or thou shalt be condemned to be foolish; thou shalt be justified to be humble, or thou shalt be condemned to be proud; thou shalt be justified to be loving, or thou shalt be condemned to be envious. Therefore Solomon saith, "A fool's lips are a snare to his own soul" (Prov. 18.7). Snares are made for other, but this snare catcheth a man's self, because it betrayeth his folly and causeth his trouble and bringeth him into discredit. Contrariwise, "The heart of the wise," saith Solomon (Prov. 17.23; Eccles. 12.10), "guideth his mouth wisely, and the words of his mouth have grace." Now, to show that this should be one mark in the choice of a wife, Solomon saith, "She openeth her mouth with wisdom, and the law of grace is in her tongue" (Prov. 19.15). . . .

The fourth sign is the apparel. For as the pride of the glutton is noted, in that he went in purple every day, so the humility of John is noted in that he went in haircloth every day. A modest woman is known by her sober attire, as the Prophet Elijah was known by his rough garment (2 Kings 1.8). Look not for better within than thou seest without; for every one seemeth better than he is, if the face be vanity, the heart is pride. He which biddeth thee abstain from the show of evil would have thee to abstain from those wives which have the shows of evil; for it is hard to come in the fashion and not to be in the abuse. And therefore Paul saith, "Fashion not yourselves like unto this world" (Rom. 12.2), as though the fashions of men did declare of what side they are.

The fifth sign is the company. For birds of a feather will fly together, and fellows in sin will be fellows in league, as young Rehoboam chose young companions (1 Kings 12). The tame beasts will not keep with the wild, nor the clean with the leprous. If a man can be known by nothing else, then he may be known by his companions; for like will to like, as Solomon saith (Prov. 1.11). (pp. 35–42)

• • •

PARENTS' CONSENT IN MARRIAGE

Now in this choice are two questions. First, whether children may marry without their parents' consent, and second, whether they may marry with papists, atheists, etc. Touching the first, God saith, "Honor thy father and thy mother" (Exod. 20). Now wherein canst thou honor them more than in this honorable action, to which they have preserved thee and brought thee up, which concerneth the state of thy whole life? . . .

The second question is answered of Paul, when he saith, "Be not unequally yoked with infidels." As we should not be yoked with infidels, so we should not be yoked with papists, and so we should not be yoked with atheists, for that also is to be unequally yoked, unless we be atheists too. As the Jews might not marry with the Canaanites, so we may not marry with them which are like Canaanites, but as the sons of Jacob said unto Emor which would marry their sister, "We may not give our sister to a man uncircumcised, but if ye will be circumcised like us, then we will marry with you" (Gen. 34.14). So parents should say to suitors, "I may not give my daughter to a man unsanctified, but if you will be sanctified, then I will give my daughter unto you." Though heresy and irreligion be not a cause of divorce, as Paul teacheth, yet it is a cause of restraint; for we may not marry at all with whom we may live being married. If adultery may separate marriage, shall not idolatry hinder marriage, which is worse than it? . . . Thy wife must be meet, as God said (Gen. 2.18). But how is she meet if thou be a Christian and she a papist? We must marry in the Lord, as Paul saith (1 Cor. 7.39); but how do we marry in the Lord when we marry the Lord's enemies? (pp. 43–50)

• • •

MARRIAGE COMPOUNDED OF TWO LOVES

In every state there is some one virtue which belongeth to that calling more than others, as justice to magistrates, and knowledge to preachers, and fortitude to soldiers: so love is the marriage virtue, which sings music to their whole life. Wedlock is made of two loves, which I may call the first love and the after-love. As every man is taught to love God before he be bid to love his neighbor, so they must love God before they can love one another.

To show the love which should be between man and wife, marriage is called *conjugium*, which signifieth a knitting or joining together: showing that unless there be a joining of hearts and knitting of affections together, it is not marriage indeed, but in show and name, and they shall dwell in a house like two poisons in a stomach, and one shall ever be sick of the other. (pp. 55–56)

• • •

DUTIES OF THE HUSBAND

The man may spell his duty out of his name, for he is called the head (Eph. 5.23): to show that as the eye and the tongue and the ear are in the head to direct the whole body, so the man should be stored with wisdom and understanding and knowledge and discretion to direct his whole family; for it is not right that the worse should rule the better, but that the better should rule the worse, as the best rules all. The husband saith that his wife must obey him because he is her better; therefore, if he let her be better than himself, he seems to free her from her obedience and bind himself to obey her.

His first duty is called *hearting*, that is, hearty affection. As they are handfasted, so they must be heartfasted; for the eye and the tongue and the hand will be her enemies if the heart be not her friend. As Christ draweth all the commandments to love, so I may draw all their duties to love, which is the heart's gift to the bride. First, he must choose his love, and then he must love his choice; this is the oil which maketh all things easy. . . .

His next duty to love is a fruit of his love, that is, to let all things be common between them which were private before. The man and the wife are partners like two oars in a boat; therefore, he must divide offices and affairs and goods with her, causing her to be feared and reverenced and obeyed of her children and servants like himself; for she is as an under-officer in his commonweal, and therefore she must be assisted and borne out like his deputy, as the prince standeth with his magistrates for his own quiet, because they are the legs which bear him up. To show this community between husband and wife, he is to maintain her as he doth himself, because Christ saith, "They are no more two but one" (Mark 10.8). . . . He may not say, as husbands are wont to say, that which is thine is mine, and that which is mine is my own: but, that which is mine is thine and myself, too. . . .

Lastly, he must tender her as much as all her friends, because he hath taken her from her friends and covenanted to tender her for them all. To show how he should tender her, Peter saith, "Honor the woman as the weaker vessel" (1 Pet. 3.7). As we do not handle glasses like pots, because they are weaker vessels, but touch them nicely and softly for fear of cracks, so a man must entreat his wife with gentleness and softness, not expecting that wisdom, nor that faith, nor that patience, nor that strength in the weaker vessel which should be in the stronger; but think when he takes a wife, he takes a vineyard, not grapes, but a vineyard to bear him grapes. Therefore, he must sow it and dress it and water it and fence it and think it a good vineyard if it at last bring forth grapes. So he must not look to find a wife without a fault but think that she is committed to him to reclaim her from her faults; for all are defectives. And if he find the proverb true, that in space cometh grace, he must rejoice as much at his wife when she mendeth as the husbandman rejoiceth when his vineyard beginneth to fructify. (pp. 61–69)

• • •

THE WOMAN'S DUTIES

Likewise, the woman may learn her duty out of her names. They are called *goodwives*, as Goodwife A. and Goodwife B. Every wife is called Goodwife; therefore, if they be not goodwives, their names do belie them, and they are not worth their titles, but answer to a wrong name, as players do upon a stage. This name pleaseth them well, but beside this a wife is called a *yoke-fellow*, to show that she should help her husband to bear his yoke; that is, his grief must be her grief, and whether it be the yoke of poverty, or the yoke of envy, or the yoke of sickness, or the yoke of imprisonment, she must submit her neck to bear it patiently with him, or else she is not his yoke-fellow but his yoke, as though she were inflicted upon him for a penalty, like Job's wife whom the devil left to torment him when he took away all beside (Job 2.9). . . .

Beside a yoke-fellow, she is called a *helper*, to help him in his business, to help him in his labors, to help him in his troubles, to help him in his sickness like a woman physician, sometime with her strength and sometime with her counsel. For sometime as God confoundeth the wife by the foolish and the strong by the weak, so he teacheth the wise by the foolish and helpeth the strong by the weak (1 Cor. 1.27). . . .

Beside a helper, she is called a *comforter* too, and therefore the man is bid to rejoice in his wife, which is as much to say, that wives be the rejoicing of their husbands, even like David's harp to comfort Saul (1 Sam. 16.23). Therefore it is said of Rebecca that she prepared meat for her husband, such as he loved (Gen. 27.9): so a good wife is known when her words and deeds and countenances are such as her husband loveth; she must not examine whether he be wise or simple, but that she is his wife, and therefore they which are bound must obey, as Abigail loved her husband though he was a fool (1 Sam. 25.3). For the wife is as much despised for taking rule over her husband as he for yielding it unto her. It becomes not the mistress to be master, no more than it beseemeth the master to be mistress, but both to sail with their own wind.

Lastly, we call the wife *Huswife*, that is, housewife; not a street wife like Tamar (Gen. 38.14), nor a field wife like Dinah (Gen. 34.1), but a housewife to show that a good wife keeps her house. And therefore Paul biddeth Titus to exhort women that they be chaste and keeping at home: presently after Christ, he saith, "keeping at home," as though home were chastity's keeper. . . . The angel asked Abraham, "Where is thy wife?" Abraham answered, "She is in the tent" (Gen. 18.9). The angel knew where she was, but yet he asked that we might see how women in old time did keep their tents and houses. . . .

As it becometh her to keep home, so it becometh her to keep silence and always speak the best of her head [i.e., husband]. Others seek their honor in triumph, but she must seek her honor in reverence, for it becometh not any woman to set light by her husband, nor to publish his infirmities. . . . Though a woman be wise and painful and have many good parts, yet if she be a shrew, her troublesome jarring in the end will make her honest behavior unpleasant, as her over-pinching at last causeth her good huswifery to be evil spoken of. Therefore, though she be a wife, yet sometime she must observe the servant's lesson, "Not answering again" (Titus 2.9), and hold her peace to keep the peace. Therefore, they which keep silence oftentimes doth keep the peace when words would break it.

To her silence and patience she must add the acceptable obedience, which makes a woman rule while she is ruled. This is the wife's tribute to the husband; for she is not called his head, but he is called her head (Eph. 5.23). Great cause hath man to make much of his wife, for great and many are her duties to him. And therefore Paul saith, "Wives, submit yourselves unto your husbands as to the Lord" (Eph. 5.22), showing that she should regard his will as the Lord's will; but withal as the Lord commandeth only that which is good and right, so she should obey her husband in good and right, or else she doth not obey him as the Lord, but as the tempter. (pp. 74–84)

QUESTIONS FOR WRITTEN AND ORAL DISCUSSION

1. Discuss Bassanio's reasons for wooing Portia. What is his primary reason? Is it her fortune, her beauty, or her character that most interests him, or a combination of all three? Are his motives consistent with what the sixteenth-century commentators say about the best reasons for getting married?

2. Discuss Portia's attitude toward her suitors in 1.2. What does she find so disagreeable about them? How does she react to her father's will? Since she is so dissatisfied with the quality of her suitors and the requirements of her father's will, why does she comply with it? What other recourse might she have?

3. Why do the Christian theologians object to intermarriage? In your opinion are their objections valid? Why does Lorenzo woo Jessica? Like his friend Bassanio, is he more interested in her money, her beauty, or her character? Why does Jessica find it necessary to elope in the disguise of a page?

4. How happy is Jessica in her conversion to Christianity? Why does Lancelot tease her so severely in 3.5 about it? What is the attitude of others toward Jessica, for example, when she arrives with Lorenzo in Belmont? Is she welcomed as an equal, or treated as an outsider?

5. Contrast Portia's and Jessica's attitude toward their fathers. Why is Jessica eager to abandon her home with Shylock? Is she justified? The Christian commentators frequently allude to the commandment, "Honor thy father and thy mother." Does Jessica violate that commandment? Compare also Lancelot's attitude toward his father. How respectful is he, and why does he want his father's blessing?

6. After Bassanio chooses the right casket, Portia yields herself and her fortune to him completely. But from what we know of her character and what happens later in the play, do you see her as a meekly compliant wife? Or will she be more in charge of family affairs than she seems to indicate at first? If so, how will she manage to do so and still remain a loyal, obedient wife, as the Protestant preachers recommend she should be?

7. Why do Henry Smith and others place such heavy emphasis on obtaining parental consent to marry? What dangers do they foresee in not consulting parents or guardians before tying the marital knot? Are they right? Should children be guided entirely by their parents' advice, even to the point of letting them choose their marriage partners? What middle ground do some of the commentators recom-

mend? Do you think Jessica is heading for trouble by not consulting Shylock in her choice of a husband?

8. What are the chief reasons for getting married, according to the Renaissance thinkers on the subject? What role do mutual love and affection play? What are the qualities in a mate that are strongly recommended as most suitable? What qualities are emphatically warned against? Do the several couples in *The Merchant of Venice* meet all of these criteria, or only some? Which ones? Discuss in detail.

9. According to Henry Smith, how should a husband treat his wife? Why does Smith compare wives to glasses and contrast them to pots? Does Graziano treat Nerissa in the way Smith urges? Does Lorenzo treat Jessica in that way? What other comparisons or contrasts can you make among the various couples that marry in *The Merchant of Venice?* Among other couples in Shakespeare's plays that you know?

10. Smith enumerates several duties that a wife must perform. Are these the best ways to insure marital bliss? Compare Portia, Nerissa, and Jessica in the way that you see them carrying out those duties. For example, how silent and patient do you think they are or will be in married life?

11. What are a husband's chief duties to his wife, as the writers in this chapter describe them? Do Bassiano, Graziano, and Lorenzo fulfill these duties? Do you see Lorenzo and Jessica, for example, as "two oars in a boat," sharing offices, affairs, and goods? What about Bassiano and Portia, Nerissa and Graziano?

12. Analyze Shakespeare's use of the ring plot. Why does he retain this part of his source? What lessons do Portia and Nerissa try to teach their husbands by it? Do they succeed? Do you think that their husbands defense of their actions in giving the rings to the doctor and his clerk is reasonable? What role does Antonio have in helping them to justify their behavior?

13. Write a sequel to act 5 in which you engage at least one of the couples in dialogue some time after their marriage. How harmoniously do they get along? What problems confront them, and how do they go about dealing with them as a couple? (You do not have to imitate Shakespearean language; you can use contemporary speech for this exercise, if you wish.)

14. Write another skit in which you imagine life in Shylock's household before his wife, Leah, died. Note what Shylock says about "the Christian husbands" (4.1.292); does he imply that Jewish husbands are different, and if so, in what ways are they different? Do you think that Shylock's lines about the ring Leah gave him suggest something about

their relationship before and after their marriage? What do you suppose happened to Jessica and Shylock after Leah died?

15. None of the children in *The Merchant of Venice* have mothers, and only two of them, Jessica and Lancelot, have living fathers. What does the absence of a wife and mother suggest in the development of their characters? In several other plays, *King Lear* for example, mothers also do not appear. What effect does Shakespeare seem to suggest by the absence of mothers in these plays? Compare the presence of mothers in other plays you have read, such as *Romeo and Juliet*.

SUGGESTED READINGS

Cook, Ann Jennalie. *Making a Match: Courtship in Shakespeare and His Society*. Princeton, NJ: Princeton University Press, 1991.

Cressy, David. *Birth, Marriage, and Death: Ritual, Religion, and the Life-Cycle in Tudor and Stuart England*. Oxford: Oxford University Press, 1997.

Hopkins, Lisa. *Shakespearean Marriage: Merry Wives and Heavy Husbands*. New York: Saint Martin's Press, 1998.

Levin, Richard A. *Love and Society in Shakespearean Comedy*. Newark: University of Delaware Press, 1985.

McMurtry, Jo. *Understanding Shakespeare's England: A Companion for the American Reader*. Hamden, CT: Shoestring Press, 1989.

Singman, Jeffrey L. *Daily Life in Elizabethan England*. Westport, CT: Greenwood Press, 1995.

Stone, Lawrence. *The Family, Sex and Marriage in England 1500–1800*. Abridged ed. New York: Harper Torchbooks, 1979.

Wrightson, Keith. *English Society, 1580–1680*. New Brunswick, NJ: Rutgers University Press, 1982.

6

Usury, Interest, and the Rise of Capitalism

The controversy over usury, lending money at interest, raged throughout early modern Europe and became especially acute during the Renaissance. Usury was regarded as unchristian, and insofar as the Church exerted its influence and considerable power, it was prohibited for centuries, until the rise of capitalistic enterprise during the Continental Renaissance felt the need for interest-bearing loans to foster trade and other business enterprises. Italian bankers, such as the Medicis in Italy, were in the forefront of those who insisted on the practice of usury as necessary for business expansion. They worked hard, therefore, to gain control of the papacy whenever possible and to circumvent the laws against usury. Others naturally followed until the practice of usury became widespread in Europe, not only among Jews who were forbidden to own land (which was the basis of wealth in the Middle Ages), but also among Christians. The period 1300–1700 is well known for the growth of the banking industry and the expansion of trade as new markets were found, especially in India and the rest of Asia, during this age of exploration.

In the Renaissance much of the controversy over usury centered upon interpretations of Scripture, the prohibitions against certain kinds of usury stipulated in several books of the Bible, but discussions of the issue actually go as far back as Plato and Aristotle. St.

Thomas Aquinas (1224 or 1225–1274) argued vigorously against any kind of usury: to pay interest on loans, he said, was forbidden, and he gave his reasons (Jones 1989, 8–10). Changing economic circumstances in the Renaissance, however, which saw the rise of banking in Italy and throughout the rest of Europe, required a different definition of usury, one that would sanction at least some kinds of moneylending at interest. The key issue became intent: what the money was borrowed for and under what circumstances it was borrowed. While some scholars and theologians maintained that any sort of interest amounted to usury, others found ways around biblical prohibitions. For example, partnerships that involved investments for potential profit could be permitted. The issue then became risk. If risk was involved, the investor could reasonably expect to be compensated. This was different from contractual loans where the amount of interest was fixed for a period of time, which amounted to usury.

Protestant reformers were not all of one mind, just as Catholics were not. Whereas Luther accepted the orthodox view that usury was a sin, a number of his followers did not. Jakob Strauss, for instance, one of the more radical reformers, maintained, in defiance of Luther, that Old Testament law was not binding upon Christians. Melancthon, too, another of Luther's followers, was not as conservative as his mentor. But both Luther and Melancthon held that secular authorities could regulate interest for the good of the community (Jones 1989, 15). Calvin moved still further away, as did the French theologian Charles du Moulin, whose arguments were anticipated as early as 1530 by Heinrich Bullinger (Baker 1974, 5:49–70). Under certain circumstances, they argued, lending at interest was permissible, for example, when it involved long-term loans at reasonable rates (no more than 5 percent). Both defended lending to the poor at no interest, though lending to the rich was permissible when it did not involve extortion or injury of any kind. The important thing was to observe the Golden Rule, "Do unto others as you would be done by."

In England in the sixteenth century these divergent views were vigorously debated, becoming a major issue in mid-century when Parliament considered a bill limiting loans at 10 percent interest. Martin Bucer, a principal figure in the debate, upheld the view that not all usury was sinful. The motivation of the loan was crucial in determining between licit and illicit interest-bearing loans. What was also important was not the interest per se but the amount of interest and the use to which the loan was put. Without lending at interest, many legitimate enterprises could not go forward, such as trade and agriculture. Thus Bucer reconciled theology and commerce, noting an important difference, as Calvin had said, between the Hebrew terms used in Scripture: *nesheck*, "biting usury," which injured one's neighbor, and *tarbith*, the taking of legitimate interest, which injured nobody.

Bucer's opponent in England, where these debates were held, was John Young, the future Master of Pembroke Hall, Cambridge, during the reign of Queen Mary (1553–1558). Young held steadfastly to the conservative view against any kind of usury. At the end, the two could agree on only two points: that much usury was sinful and to be deplored, and that money could be lent at interest for charitable purposes, as in Italy where the *Monti di Pietà* were established as lending agencies to the poor that charged little or no interest.

Although some in England found Bucer's view of usury attractive, many others adhered to the older definition of usury and held it a sin (Jones 1989, 25). The issue came to a head in 1571 when Parliament considered the Act against Usury. Members could not separate faith and law. Dr. Thomas Wilson, author of *A Discourse upon Usury* (1572), and John Jewel, Bishop of Salisbury, led the conservative faction against usury of any kind. Although both were staunch Protestants, in this instance they followed orthodox canon law, as derived from Aquinas. Jewel preached in his sermons that all usury was evil; there was no such thing as "beneficial" usury. All loans at interest were extortionate and oppressive and violated the commandment to love thy neighbor.

Opposing the conservatives were those in the House of Commons, like John Woolley, the Queen's Latin Secretary, who were influenced by the "French" school of thought on usury, imported by Bucer in mid-century. For them usury was a sin when the borrower and lender were out of charity with one another, that is, one or the other sought unfair advantage (Jones 1989, 29–30). They echoed the views of Master Lawyer, the antagonist in Wilson's *Discourse*, who held that not all usury is wicked, only that which is "biting and oversharp." Lending to the rich by the rich, where both parties gained, was not usurious. (This point overlooked the argument of conservatives like Jewel, who astutely noted that in such cases a loss was borne by the consumer.) Excess, not gain, was the problem that required redress. Covetousness, not usury, was the damnable sin.

The total prohibition against usury, passed during the reign of Edward VI in 1552, did more harm than good, in practical terms, as it drove up the price of money and seriously handicapped English merchants involved in trade with other countries (Jones 1989, 33; Wilson n.d., 155–56). Moreover, to encourage industriousness, one had to adhere to the profit motive. What the argument came down to was that the state should regulate the rate of interest, leaving it to God, who alone knows the secret of men's hearts, to determine the motivation and morality of the lender. Lord Burghley, Lord Treasurer of England under Elizabeth I, studied all aspects of the problem, both religious and pragmatic, and finally determined that the harmful effects of usury were such that moneylending required regulation; thus, he supported the 1571 act, which tolerated lending at interest without sanctioning usury per se.

According to Jones (1989, 43), the opposing sides could agree that usury was wrong and had a deleterious effect upon society, but they could not agree on precisely what usury was or what they should do about it. Perhaps the most injurious effect, many believed, was the social mobility that usury promoted (i.e., the ability of people to rise above their class by making money through usury). This mobility upset the social hierarchy and could lead to anarchy, as gentlemen (born to wealth and entitled to bear arms) were reduced to poverty by grasping usurers, who rose in their place. Nevertheless, throughout Europe, princes used civil law to regulate usury, not abolish it (Jones 1989, 58). After vigorous debate in both houses of Parliament, a bill was approved that revived in essence the act of 1545 under Henry VIII, which allowed interest at no more than 10 percent, but which was now carefully circumscribed by various restrictions and enhanced enforcement. Offenders faced penalties of triple their principal, for example, half going to the crown and half to the informer. The act, labeled "Against Usury," was a compromise between the conservative and the more liberal members of Parliament. It tilted toward the conservative interpretation of usury, however, by stating in part that the statute "shall be most largely and strongly construed for the repression of usury and against all persons that shall offend against the true meaning of the said statute by any way or device, directly or in-directly."

Whatever the intent of the act and despite its ambivalence—or, more likely, because of it—lending at interest remained wide-spread, and through various strategems some abuses continued (Greaves 1981, 598–99). Interest rates tended to fluctuate with lenders and borrowers during Elizabeth's reign, while powerful clergymen continued to sermonize against usury. Nevertheless, the act was not repealed, and by the time of James I's accession in 1603, 10 percent had become the normal rate. Although usury was never made legal, it was regulated, not an uncommon paradox in the Age of Elizabeth. The statute of 1571 remained in effect until 1624, when interest was limited to 8 percent.

The initial antagonism between Antonio and Shylock in *The Merchant of Venice* centers on the issue of usury. Whereas Antonio follows the orthodox view and never borrows or lends money at interest (1.3.58–59), Shylock's business is precisely that. Shylock defends his practice by invoking at one point the story of Jacob and Laban, or the way Jacob made his share of the flocks increase while serving his father-in-law and preparing to go off on his own (1.3.68–87). The analogy is inexact, and Shylock tries to make a joke of it, but his underlying point is a serious one: "This was a way to thrive, and he was blest; / And thrift is blessing, if men steal it not" (86–87). For Shylock, lending at interest is "thrift"; for Antonio, it is usury, against which he has often railed (1.3.45–48). In the past he has earned Shylock's enmity not only for that, but also for delivering out of his hands debtors who owed Shylock money and were unable to pay it back (3.3.21–24). Antonio has "hindered me half a million," Shylock complains; "laughed at my losses, mocked at my gains, scorned my nation, thwarted my bargains, cooled my friends, heated mine enemies" (3.1.52–54). Moreover, by lending money at no interest, Antonio has brought down the rate of usury in Venice (1.3.41–42). No wonder the two are ene-mies.

It is extraordinary, therefore, that when Antonio has to find money to subsidize his friend Bassanio's expedition to Belmont, he must resort to Shylock and his usurious ways. Shylock is fully aware of the situation and makes no bones about it, reminding Antonio how he has often angrily rebuked him in the Rialto about his moneys and his usuances, which he has nevertheless always borne "with a patient shrug" (1.3.103–6). It is more extraordinary still that when it comes down to it, Shylock is willing to lend the required 3,000 ducats to Antonio *at no interest* whatever. Whether Shylock is trying by this means to ingratiate himself with Antonio, letting bygones be bygones to win his friendship, as he claims (1.3.134–38), or whether he has a more sinister motive—to "catch him once upon the hip" (i.e., at a disadvantage) (1.3.43)—is not clear. Very likely both motives influence Shylock here, contradictory though they may be. (See Chapter 1 for a discussion of the many contradictions and inconsistencies in the play.) In any event, the controversy over usury, while not as virulent as it had been some decades earlier, was still an issue at the end of the sixteenth century in England, although many Elizabethans, including Shakespeare himself, engaged in lending money or other commodities at interest. Capitalism was progressing apace, superseding the older feudal economy. If it took a little longer to arrive and take hold in England, by the eighteenth and nineteenth centuries that nation was the leader among nations in capitalist enterprises.

THE CONTROVERSY OVER USURY IN THE SIXTEENTH CENTURY

The following extracts, beginning with the relevant verses from Scripture, provide the religious, political, and social contexts for the controversy regarding usury. The amount of literature published in the sixteenth century testifies to the importance of the issue, and only a fraction of it can be included here. Shakespeare and his contemporaries could not help but be aware of the various points of view as they were discussed and debated, and as they influenced their everyday lives. For the Age of Elizabeth was, like our own, a very litigious period, and many went to court to sue for what may seem like paltry sums. Those who were unable to repay their debts often found themselves in prison, their plight decried by Phillip Stubbes in his *Anatomy of Abuses*, and later in the nineteenth century, by writers like Charles Dickens. The sight of citizens like Antonio being led off to prison (3.3) was not an uncommon event in Shakespeare's London.

Of the many Bibles that circulated in the later sixteenth century in England, the Geneva Bible was the most popular. Shakespeare read and alluded to it frequently, although he was familiar with others, such as the Bishops' Bible published in 1568. He read not only the text, but the marginal glosses, or annotations, for which the Geneva Bible is deservedly famous.

FROM THE GENEVA BIBLE (1560)

Exodus 22.25:
If thou lend money to my people, that is, to the poor with thee, thou shalt not be as an usurer unto him: ye shall not oppress him with usury.

Leviticus 25:35–37:
Moreover, if thy brother be impoverished and fallen in decay with thee, thou shalt relieve him and as a stranger and a sojourner, so shall he live with thee.

Thou shalt take no usury of him nor vantage, but thou shalt fear thy God, that thy brother may live with thee.

Thou shalt not give him thy money to usury, nor lend him thy victuals for increase.

Deuteronomy 23.19–20:

Thou shalt not give to usury to thy brother, as usury of money, usury of meat, usury of anything that is put to usury.

Unto a stranger thou mayest lend upon usury, but thou shalt not lend upon usury unto thy brother, that the Lord thy God may bless thee in all that thou setteth thine hand to, in the land whither thou goest to possess it.

Proverbs 28.8:

He that increaseth his riches by usury and interest gathereth them for him that will be merciful to the poor. [Marginal gloss: For God will take away the wicked usurer and give his goods to him that shall bestow them well.]

Psalm 15.5:

He that giveth not his money unto usury, nor taketh reward against the innocent: he that doeth these things shall never be moved. [Marginal gloss: That is, shall not be cast forth of the church as hypocrites.]

(See also Ezekiel 18, especially verses 8, 13–17; and Chapter 22, especially verses 12–13.)

Luke 6.30–36:

Give to every man that asketh of thee; and of him that taketh away thy goods, ask them not again.

And as ye would that men should do to you, so do ye to them likewise.

For if ye love them which love you, what thank shall ye have? For even the sinners love those that love them.

And if ye do good for them which do good for you, what thank shall ye have? For even the sinners do the same.

And if ye lend to them of whom ye hope to receive, what thank shall ye have? For even the sinners lend to sinners to receive the like.

Wherefore, love ye your enemies and do good, looking for nothing again, and your reward shall be great, and ye shall be of the children of the Most High: for He is kind to the unkind and to the evil.

Be ye therefore merciful, as your Father is also merciful.

The Act against Usury, passed early in Elizabeth I's reign (1558–1603), superseded the act abolishing the practice of usury that Paliament established during the reign of Edward VI (1547–53). While it restored the provision of the act that had been in effect since the time of Henry VIII by allowing interest at a maximum of 10 percent, it also tried to suppress the more objectionable aspects of usury; hence, the title of the act. This act continued to be the law of the land well into the next century and thus was operative during Shakespeare's time and the composition of *The Merchant of Venice*. The language is legalese, or lawyer's language, and typically uses a series of terms to try to avoid ambiguity. The language may be difficult at first to understand, though the main points emerge clearly enough. Despite its pious purpose, the act takes cognizance of the actual world of affairs and is realistic in its provisions.

FROM AN ACT AGAINST USURY (1571)

Whereas the Parliament held the seventh and thirty year of the reign of our late sovereign, Lord King Henry the Eighth of famous memory, there was then made and established one good act for the reformation of usury; by which act the vice of usury was well repressed, and specially the corrupt chevisance [i.e., lending] and bargaining by way of sale of wares and shifts of interest; and where since that time by one other act made in the fifth and sixth years of the reign of our late sovereign Lord King Edward the Sixth, the said former act was repealed and new provisos for repressing the usury devised and enacted; which said latter act hath not done so much good as was hoped it should, but rather the said vice of usury, and specially by way of sale of wares and shifts of interest hath much more exceedingly abounded to the utter undoing of many gentlemen, merchants, occupiers, and others, and to the impossible hurt of the commonwealth, as well for that in the said latter act there is no provision against such corrupt shifts and sales of wares, as also for that there is no difference of pain, forfeiture, or punishment upon the greater or lesser exactions and oppressions by reason of loans upon usury: Be it therefore enacted, That the said latter statute made in the fifth and sixth years of the reign of King Edward the Sixth, and every branch and article of the same, from and after the five and twenty day of June next coming, shall be utterly abrogated, repealed, and made void; and that the said act made in the said seven and thirty year of King Henry the Eighth, from and after the said five and twenty day of June next coming, shall be revived and stand in full force, strength, and effect.

And be it further enacted, That all bonds, contracts, and assurances, collateral, or other, to be made for payment of any principal or money to be lent, or covenant to be performed upon, or for any usury in lending or doing of anything against the said act now revived, upon or by which loan or doing there, shall be reserved or taken above the rate of ten pounds for the hundred for one year, shall be utterly void.

And be it further enacted, That all brokers, solicitors, and drivers of bargains for contracts or other doings against the said statute now revived, whereupon shall be reserved or taken more than after the rate of ten pounds for the loan of a hundred pounds a year, shall be to all intents and purposes judged, punished, and used as counselors, attorneys, or advocates in any case of praemunire [i.e., support of papal jurisdiction].

And for as much as all usury being forbidden by the law of God is sin and destestable, Be it enacted, That all usury, loan, and forbearing of money, or giving of days for forbearing of money by way of loan, chevisance [lending], shifts, sale of wares, contract, or other doings whatsoever for gain mentioned in the said statute which is now revived, whereupon is not reserved or taken or covenanted to be reserved, paid, or given to the lender, contractor, shifter, forbearer, or deliverer above the sum of ten pounds for the loan or forbearing of a hundred pounds for one year, or after that rate for a more or lesser sum of time, shall be from the five and twenty day of June coming, punished in form following; that is to say, That every such offender against this branch of this present statute shall forfeit so much as shall be reserved by way of usury above the principal for any money so to be lent or forborn; all such forfeitures to be recovered and employed as is limited by forfeitures by the said former statute now revived.

And be it further enacted, That Justices of Oyer and Terminer and Justices of Assize in their circuits, Justices of Peace in their sessions, mayors, sheriffs, and bailiffs of cities shall also have full power and authority to inquire, hear, and determine of all and singular offences committed against the said statute now revived.

And be it further enacted, That the said statute now revived shall be most largely and strongly construed for the repressing of usury, and against all persons that shall offend against the true meaning of the said statute by any way or device, directly or indirectly. . . .

The debate on the Act against Usury is from the manuscript of a journal by an anonymous person but regarded by historians as sufficiently accurate and authentic as to give a good record of proceedings. John Woolley (d. 1596), as Latin Secretary to Queen Elizabeth, became a member of the Privy Council in 1586 and was appointed one of the commissioners to try Mary, Queen of Scots. From 1571 to the end of his life he was a member of every Parliament called by Elizabeth I and was knighted in 1592. His wife, Elizabeth, was a lady of the privy chamber to the Queen.

FROM JOHN WOOLLEY'S SPEECH IN PARLIAMENT
(April 17, 1571)
(See *Proceedings in the Parliaments of Elizabeth I: 1558–1581*, Ed.
T. E. Hartley; Leicester: Leicester University Press, 1981)

Mr. Woolley . . . showed what it might be thought of for any man to endeavor the defence of that which every preacher at all times, following the letter of the book, doth preach against. Yet, said he, it is convenient and being in some sort used is not repugnant to the word of God. Experience hath proved the great mischief which doth grow by reason of excessive taking to the destruction of young gentlemen, and otherwise infinitely; but the mischief is of the excess, and not otherwise, since to take reasonable, or so that both parties might do good, was not hateful; for to have any man to lend his money without commodity, hardly should you bring that to pass. And since every man is not an occupier [i.e., dealer] that hath money, and some such indeed who hath not money yet may have skill to use money, except you should take away or hinder good trades, bargaining, and contracting, it cannot be. God did not so hate it that he did utterly forbid it, but to the Jews among themselves only, for that he willed that they should live as brethren together; for unto all others they were at large, and therefore to this day they are the greatest usurers in the world. But be it as it is indeed evil, and that men are men and no saints to do all things perfectly, uprightly, or brotherly, yet . . . better may it be borne to permit a little than to take away and prohibit all traffic, which hardly may be maintained generally without this. But it will be said it is contrary to the express word of God and therefore an ill law. If it were to appoint men to take usury, it were to be disliked; but the difference is great between that and permitting or allowing and suffer a matter to pass unpunished. . . . We are not . . . so straitened to the word of God that every transgression should be severely punished here: every vain word is forbidden by God, yet the temporal law doth not so utterly condemn it. As for the words of Scripture . . . it is the biting and oversharp dealing which is disliked, and nothing else. And this, he said, was the mind and interpretation of the most famous learned man, Beza, in these days, and of one Bellarmine, who said that the true interpretation of the Hebrew word is not *usura* [interest] but *morsus* [biting]. (pp. 231–32)

Thomas Wilson (1525?–1581) is best known for his important works on logic and rhetoric, especially *The Arte of Rhetorique* (1553). Educated at Eton and Cambridge, he became active in politics and was twice elected to Parliament. He also served as secretary of state from 1577 to 1580, after which he became dean of Durham Cathedral. His *Discourse upon Usury* is an important document in the controversy that raged in the early decades of Elizabeth's reign. Note especially Wilson's commentary on the verses in Scripture that pertain to usury, which became the focal points for commentaries by many others during this period, and his remarks about Jews as usurers, who likewise preoccupied commentators. Although he is certainly against usury, Wilson can see both sides of the issue, as he presents them in the orations by the Preacher and the Lawyer in his *Discourse*.

FROM THOMAS WILSON, *A DISCOURSE UPON USURY* (1572)
(Ed. R. H. Tawney; New York: Harcourt Brace, n.d.)

FROM "THE PREACHER'S ORATION"

To lend freely is a kind of liberality and bountifulness, when a man departeth from his own to help his neighbor's want, without any hope of lucre or gain at all; for he is benefited that borroweth and feeleth great comfort in his great need. Whereas lending for gain is a chief branch of covetousness, and makes him that before might have been counted bountiful to be now reckoned a greedy gainer for himself, seeking his own welfare upon good assurance, without any care at all what becometh of his neighbor, gnawing him unmercifully, to satisfy his own wretched and most greedy hunger, directly turning a most beautiful virtue into a most filthy abominable vice. Yea, usury is a manifest and voluntary known theft, which men do use knowingly and wittingly, for either they think they do evil and forbear it never a whit, or (that which is worse of all) they think they do well, and so, by oft using of this filthiness, do lull themselves in sin without any sense of feeling or their most wretched wickedness and horrible dealing. Christ for his bitter passion be merciful unto us and gave us his fear, that we may live after his law and follow his holy will; for surely, as we live now, either the bible is not God's word, or else we are not of God, such contrariety is between our lives and our lessons.

The scripture commandeth: Thou shalt not steal; Thou shalt not kill; Thou shalt not commit adultery; Thou shalt not bear false witness; Thou shalt not lend out thy money for gain, to take anything for the loan of it. And yet we do all these things, as though they were neither scripture that forbade us, nor heaven for us to desire, nor hell to eschew, nor God to honor, nor devil to dread. And this last horrible offence, which I count greater, or as great, as any of the rest, is so common amongst us, that we have no sense to take it for sin, but count it lawful bargaining and judge them goodly wise men that, having great masses of money by them, will never adventure any jot thereof in lawful occupying [i.e., dealing], either to carry out our plenty, or to bring in our want, as good merchants use and ought to do; but living idle at home, will set out their money for profit and so enrich themselves with the labor and travail of others, being themselves none other than drones that suck the honey which other painful bees gather with their continual travail of divers flowers in every field. And whether these men be profitable or tolerable to a commonweal or no, I report me to you. Besides that, God doth utterly forbid them, whose commandment ought to be obeyed, if we be Christians and of God, as we profess to be.

And therefore for my part, I will wish some penal law of death to be made against those usurers, as well as against thieves and murderers, for that they deserve death much more than such men do; for these usurers destroy and devour up not only whole families, but also whole countries, and bring all folk to beggary that have to do with them, and therefore are much worse than thieves or murderers, because their offence hurteth more universally and toucheth a greater number, the one offending for need, the other upon wilfulness. And that which is worse, under the color of friendship, men's throats are cut and the doers counted for honest and wise men amongst others that have so ungodly gathered goods together. What is the matter that Jews are so universally hated wherever they come? Forsooth, usury is one of the chief causes, for they rob all men that deal with them, and undo them in the end. And for this cause they were hated in England and so banished worthily, with whom I would all these Englishmen were sent that lend their money or their goods whatsoever for gain; for I take them to be no better than Jews. Nay, shall I say: they are worse than Jews. For whither you will throughout Christendom and deal with them, and you shall have under ten in the hundred, yea sometimes for six at their hands, whereas English usurers exceed all God's mercy and will take they care not how much, without respect had to the party that borroweth, what loss, what danger, hindrance soever the borrower sustaineth. And how can these men be of God that are so far from charity that care not how they get goods so they may have them? (pp. 231–32)

FROM "THE LAWYER'S ORATION"

Some there be that say all usury is against nature, whereas I think clean contrary. For if usury were against nature, it should be universally evil. But God hath said that to a stranger man may put out his money for usury; but if it had been against nature, God would not have granted that liberty. So that I take it to agree both with law and nature that I should do good unto him that doth good unto me, or else I should be unthankful; than which there cannot be a greater or more horrible fault upon earth. And rewards given for good turns done or pleasure received for benefits bestowed are so common that whoso offendeth herein is pointed at and counted a churl and shall have want when he would have. Moreover, who may not give his own freely, or what is he that will not or may not take anything that is given? What is more free than a gift? Or what is he that will show such discourtesy not to receive a gift when it is freely offered? And what other thing do they that seek to borrow money, but entreat marvelously and offer frankly for the time and use of money? Moreover, it is not against the Roman laws of the emperors, but rather allowed, not only suffered, as your master doctor can best tell, by laws of your code and made by the emperor Justinian, the best prince that ever lived. Yea, the canon law itself seemeth to suffer it in the title of usury, as you know better than I can tell. Even in God's law, if I be not deceived, usury is not forbidden. For is it not in St. Luke's gospel that God said He would come and ask the money lent with the usury, blaming him that did not put it forth for gain? And in Deuteronomy it is plain: Thou shalt not lend to thy brother for gain, but to a stranger.

The common law of England is not against all usury, neither in such sort and so precisely as you take usury. And statutes there have been that have permitted usury, which I would they had continued, to avoid further evil; for (as we say) better it is to suffer a mischief than an inconvenience. But, to reason this matter further, if I lend unto a man my plate for five or six months, I may lawfully take gain only for the loan, and no man will say black is mine eye. And yet if I do take for money, by and by they will make an outcry and call men usurers therefore, whereat I marvel greatly. For a man (as I take it) may more benefit himself with an hundred marks in money than he can do with another man's basin or ewer of an hundred marks value. And yet lending of money is called usury, and lending of plate for gain to have the same plate again is no usury at all. Yet further, if I lend one a thousand pound, for pomp sake only to show at the bank (as they use in Italy and other countries), or otherwise to make some believe they have so much of their own, it is not denied but I may receive gain for the same, having my principal returned unto me in the same form and manner as I did lend it. And yet if I should have lent so much money of good will and suffered the party to occupy the same for his own benefit, restoring unto me the value thereof with some overplus or gain, then by and by I should be called an usurer. And what if one, I pray you, be an occupier [i.e., trader, dealer], and wanting money to come to me that am an occupier also and desire to borrow largely? If I bargain with him to have part of his gain, if he make any, or otherwise do covenant that if the lending of this shall be any hindrance to my occupying to get some bargain, which I shall perhaps miss, and prove it plainly, because my money is out of my hand, may I not in both these cases take usury without danger of the law or offence to God? Yes, without doubt, I may.

And yet to lend money simply is counted usury, whereas there is no man that lendeth but sustaineth loss for the want of it, because he might better benefit himself by employing it in divers ways than to suffer it to be in another man's hands, besides the danger that may happen when a man's money is out of his own hands. For surer it cannot be than in a man's own possession. Then away with this preciseness, on God's name, to make every lending for gain to be plain usury, and that one penny over is sin before God, which neither I nor yet master merchant here can well believe fully; for I would have all things weighed by reason in matters of contracts and bargains, and so not to mince things as though there were no mean.

For I do not take usury to be as whoredom or theft is. In these sins, there is no mean to make any virtue; for he that offendeth but once in whoredom is an offender, and he that stealeth never so little is a thief, and neither of their doings in any respect of circumstance is or can be good, whereas lending of money or other goods for gain may be very beneficial to him that borroweth. As for example: a man is bound to pay 300 pounds at a certain day, or else he loseth 40 pounds good land. Were it not charity and a good deed to help this man, that his land should not be lost forever? and none offence neither, as I take it, to do a good turn and to receive another.

I will go nearer. Be it there were a great dearth of corn [i.e., grain] and I have plenty lying by me, were it not better for me charitably to lend corn to the poor and needy for their sustenance and relief, and so to receive somewhat in gain at the year's end, than to suffer them to want and utterly to perish? Of two evils, the less is to be preferred; that is, better it were to lend for gain than to suffer my even Christian to die for hunger. And if I be not deceived, this is St. Augustine's opinion, who alloweth of gain in such time of necessity rather than the people should starve. . . . And, as I understand, there be of your doctors who write upon the canon law that affirm the lesser evil to be chosen before the greater, yea, even in that case of dearth and extreme famine.

Therefore, I am still of this mind, when none hath harm but both receive benefits, there is none offence committed, but rather great goodness used. (pp. 237–39)

John Calvin was born in France in 1509 but later settled in Geneva, where he joined the Genevan reform movement. He was a leading Protestant reformer, whose influence spread widely.

Among his most noted contributions to Protestant theology is his doctrine of salvation through divine election. Although he probably had little or no contact with Jews, who had been expelled from France and Geneva, Calvin doubtless was influenced by Christian teaching of contempt for the Jews. Unlike Luther, he legitimized usury (and was attacked for it by Anglican divines among others), but in his sermons and commentaries he regarded it as excessive and tyrannical (Robinson 1992, 17–20, 92).

An important distinction that Calvin makes, among others, is the difference between lending to the poor, which should not involve taking interest, and lending to the rich, which may involve taking interest, since they can afford it more easily. Calvin therefore argues for "the rule of charity." He further distinguishes between the spiritual law and the judicial law. When discussing loans made by Jews to other Jews and those made to Gentiles, as Scripture prescribed, Calvin notes that conditions are now different; the "wall of partition," he says, that separated peoples has broken down, and such distinctions no longer obtain. Compare the modern commentary in the Hebrew Bible by the late chief rabbi of Britain, Dr. J. H. Hertz: "The permission [in Deut. 23.21] to exact interest from a foreigner applied to sums only borrowed for mercantile purposes. When the Gentile needed the money for his subsistence, there was no longer any difference between Israelite and foreigner." He cites in this connection Lev. 25.35–36.

FROM JOHN CALVIN, *COMMENTARIES ON THE LAST BOOKS OF MOSES* (1554)
(Trans. C. W. Bingham; Edinburgh: Calvin Translation Society, 1854)

On Exod. 22.25: If thou lend money to any of my people (III.126–33):

Humanity ought to be very greatly regarded in the matter of loans. . . . The question here is not as to usury, as some have falsely thought, as if He commanded us to lend gratuitously, and without any hope of gain; but since in lending, private advantage is most generally sought, and therefore we neglect the poor, and only lend our money to the rich, from whom we expect some compensation, Christ reminds us that, if we seek to acquire the favour of the rich, we afford in this way no proof of our charity or mercy; and hence He proposes another sort of liberality, which is plainly gratuitous, in giving assistance to the poor, not only because our loan is a perilous one, but because they cannot make a return in kind. . . .

A precept is added as to lending without interest, which, although it is a political law, still depends on the rule of charity; inasmuch as it can scarcely happen but that the poor should be entirely drained by the exaction of interest, and that their blood should be almost sucked away. Nor had God any other object in view, except that mutual and brotherly affection should prevail amongst the Israelites. It is plain that this was a part of the Jewish polity, because it was lawful to lend at interest to the Gentiles, which distinction the spiritual law does not admit. The judicial law, however, which God prescribed to His ancient people, is only so far abrogated as that what charity dictates should remain, i.e. that our brethren, who need our assistance, are not to be treated harshly. Moreover, since the wall of partition, which formerly separated Jew and Gentile, is now broken down, our condition is now different; and consequently we must spare all without exception, both as regards taking interest even towards strangers. . . .

As touching the political law, no wonder that God should have permitted His people to receive interest from the Gentiles, since otherwise a just reciprocity would not have been preserved. . . . God commands His people not to practice usury, and still lays the Jews alone, and not foreign nations, under the obligation of this law. In order, therefore, that equality (*ratio analogica*) might be preserved, He accords the same liberty to His people which the Gentiles would assume to themselves; for this is the only intercourse that can be endured, when the condition of both parties is similar and equal. For when Plato asserts that usurers are not to be tolerated in a well-ordered republic, he does not go further than to enjoin, that its citizens should abstain from that base and dishonest traffic between each other.

The question now is, whether usury is evil in itself; and surely that which heathens even have detested appears to be by no means lawful to the children of God. We know that the name of usurer has everywhere and always been infamous and detested. Thus, Cato, desiring to commend agriculture, says that thieves were formerly condemned to a fine of double, and usurers quadruple; from which he infers, that the latter were deemed the worst. And when asked what he thought of usury, he replied, "What do I think of killing a man?" whereby he wished to show that it was as improper to make money by usury as to commit murder. This was the saying of one private individual, yet it is derived from the opinions of almost all nations and persons. And assuredly from this cause great tumults often arose at Rome, and fatal contentions were awakened between the common people and the rich; since it can hardly be but that usurers suck men's blood like leeches. . . .

But if we would form an equitable judgment, reason does not suffer us to admit that all usury is to be condemned without exception. If the debtor have protracted the time by false pretences to the loss and inconvenience of his creditor, will it be consistent that he should reap advantage from his bad faith and broken promises? Certainly no one, I think, will deny that usury ought to be paid to the creditor in addition to the principal, to compensate his loss. (I know they call this Interest, but this is all the same to me.) . . . Nor will that subtle argument of Aristotle avail, that usury is unnatural, because money is barren and does not beget money; for such a cheat as I have spoken of might make much profit by trading with another man's money. . . . But those who think differently may object, that we must abide by God's judgment, when He generally prohibits usury to His people. I reply, that the question is only as to the poor, and consequently, if we have to do with the rich, that usury is freely permitted; because the Lawgiver, in alluding to one thing, seems not to condemn another, concerning which He is silent. If again they object that usurers are absolutely condemned by David and Ezekiel (Ps. 15.5; Ez. 18.13), I think that their declarations ought to be judged by the rule of charity; and therefore that only those unjust exactions are condemned whereby the creditor, losing sight of equity, burdens and oppresses his debtor. . . . It is abundantly clear that the ancient people were prohibited from usury, but we must needs confess that this was part of their political constitution. Hence, it follows that usury is not now unlawful, except insofar as it contravenes equity and brotherly union. . . . [T]o exercise the trade of usury, since heathen writers accounted it amongst disgraceful and base modes of gain, is much less tolerable among the children of God; but in what cases, and how far it may be lawful to receive usury upon loans, the law of equity will better prescribe than any lengthened discussions.

Yehiel Nissim da Pisa (1507–1574) lived in Florence, Italy. His work, *The Eternal Life*, had never been published in its entirety until Gilbert Rosenthal's critical edition, both in Hebrew and in English translation, appeared in 1962. In 1559, Nissim da Pisa wrote his treatise on usury because the practice of lending money to Gentiles had spread widely in Italy since the rise of banking and moneylending, mostly carried on by Christians (despite the opposition of the church), had grown tremendously over the past century and a half. Since Jews had been drawn into the profession for a variety of reasons (e.g., they could not own land or join the craft guilds), rabbis in Italy and elsewhere became concerned about the practice of usury, both as it was carried on between Jew and Jew and between Jew and Christian. Actually, this concern reflects a problem that rabbis had wrestled with for centuries, as Nissim da Pisa indicates with many references throughout his tractate. The following excerpt is from Chapter 10, explaining the various prohibitions against lending at interest.

FROM YEHIEL NISSIM DA PISA, *THE ETERNAL LIFE* (1559)
(See *Banking and Finance among Jews in Renaissance Italy*,
Trans. Gilbert S. Rosenthal; New York: Bloch, 1962)

CH. 10: IN EXPLANATION OF THOSE TO WHOM IT IS PROHIBITED TO LEND ON INTEREST

Interest which is proscribed by the Torah is that which is lent from one Jew to another Jew, as it is written, "Thou shalt not lend on interest to thy brother" (Deut. 23.20). This means that anyone who enters into the realm of the Torah of Moses and takes upon himself the yoke of God's commandments, even if he be originally a gentile and subsequently became a righteous proselyte, is in the category of "thy brother" and one may not lend him upon interest. However, one may lend on interest to a gentile, for the Torah has specifically permitted such a practice by stating, "Unto a foreigner thou may lend upon interest" (Deut. 23.21). Though we say one may not defraud a gentile, one may lend him on interest since he has voluntarily and of his own accord chosen to pay the sum. The codifiers are divided on this point: Maimonides counted this amongst the positive commandments and indeed, he listed it in his *Book of the Precepts* as precept 198. We quote from his book:

> Precept 198 teaches us that God commanded us to require interest from a gentile and then we may lend to him . . . for God has commanded us, "Unto a foreigner thou may lend upon interest," and this is a positive commandment. . . .

To be sure, Rabbi Moses of Coucy and others did not count this among the positive precepts, but have declared it to be merely a permissive act, that is, when one lends to a gentile, one may receive interest from him. Since our Talmud is the basic law, it refutes the opinion that the lending of money on interest to a gentile is a positive commandment. In the Gemara Metsia [i.e., part of the Talmud] it is written: "Cannot one do without [lending on interest to gentiles]?" That is to say, must one be compelled to take interest from non-Jews? Indeed, the lender has the option to take it, for no one can force him to do so. However, in regard to a Jew, since this is a negative precept derived from a general positive precept, it becomes a positive precept. . . . This has all been analyzed by

Rabbi Moses of Coucy. . . . This is also the opinion of Rabenu Bahia, of blessed memory, in his commentary on the Torah, Chapter *Ki Tetse* [i.e., Deut. 23]. My opinion is that this is merely a permissive act and even though the Torah permitted it, our sages prohibited us from lending to gentiles on interest as a precautionary measure. They later eased the law so that we may lend to gentiles in order to make a living. In our times, it is the practice to permit lending on interest to gentiles for more than a mere living. In all of the nations of Christendom, the practice of lending money is as widespread as other business enterprises.

Blessed be He who chose them and their teachings and who foresaw what would result from lending on interest to gentiles. It is quite clear that as a result of the habit of lending to gentiles, these people fall into the error of lending on interest and usury to Jews. They can no longer distinguish between truth and falsehood or between the permitted and prohibited practices because habit is a powerful force that makes a great impression on the beliefs of people. (pp. 89–91)

Phillip Stubbes (1555?–1610?) was educated at Cambridge and Oxford but took a degree from neither university. He preferred to roam about the country, getting his education from his travels or, as his surrogate speaker Philoponus says,

> to see fashions and acquaint myself with natures, qualities, properties, and conditions of all men; to break myself to the world; to learn nature, good demeanor, and civil behavior; to see the goodly situation of cities, towns, and countries, with their prospects and commodities; and finally to learn the state of all things in general, all which I could never have learned in one place. (*Anatomy of Abuses*, B1v)

The full title of his most famous book, from which the following excerpt is taken, is *The Anatomy of Abuses: Containing a Discovery, or Brief Summary, of such Notable Vices and Imperfections as now Reign in Many Countries of the World, but (especially) in a Famous Island called Ailgna [i.e., Anglia]: Together with the most Fearful Examples of God's Judgments Executed upon the Wicked for the same, as well in Ailgna of late as in Other Places, Elsewhere*. It is written in the form of a dialogue between two interlocutors, or speakers: Spudeus and his friend Philoponus, recently returned from living in Ailgna, where he spent seven years traveling around the country. Although Stubbes was not a clergyman, he inveighed like any puritan against what he considered the vices of his time, including the theater and other unholy occupations, as in his objections to the practice of usury, and he exhibited prejudice toward Jews that was typical of his time. In discussing usury, Philoponus seems to allude to the Act against Usury (1571) and its provisious in England.

FROM PHILLIP STUBBES, *THE ANATOMY OF ABUSES* (1583)

GREAT USURY IN AILGNA

Philo. It is as impossible for any to borrow money there (for the most part) without usury and loan, or without some good hostage, gage or pledge, as it is for a dead man to speak with audible voice.

Spud. I have heard say, that the positive and statute laws there do permit them to take usury, limiting them how much to take for every pound.

Philo. Although the civil laws (for the avoiding of further inconveniences) do permit certain sums of money to be given overplus beyond or above the principal, for the loan of money lent; yet are the usurers no more discharged from the guilt of usury before God thereby than the adulterous Jews were from whoredom, because Moses gave them a permissive law for every man to put away their wives, that would, for every light trifle. And yet the laws there give no liberty to commit usury, but seeing how much it rageth, lest it should exceed, rage further, and overflow the banks of all reason and godliness—as covetousness is a raging sea and bottomless pit and never satisfied nor contented—they have limited them within certain meres [i.e., boundaries] and banks (to bridle the insatiable desires of covetous men) beyond the which it is not lawful for any man to go. But this permission of the laws argueth not that it is lawful to take usury, no more (I say) than the permission of Moses argued that whoredom and adultery is lawful and good because Moses permitted them to put away their wives for the avoiding of greater evil. For as Christ said to Jews from the beginning it was not so, so say I to these usurers from the beginning it was not so, nor yet ought to be.

Spud. If no interest were permitted, then no man would lend, and then how should the poor do? Wherefore the laws permit some small overplus therein do very well.

Philo. *Non faciendum est malum, ut inde veniat bonum*: we must not do evil that good may come of it. Yet the laws permitting certain reasonable gain to be received for the loan of money lent, lest otherwise the poor should quail (for without some commodity the rich would not lend) have not done much amiss; but if they had quite cut it off and not yielded at all to any such permission, they had done better. But herein the intent of the law is to be perpended: which was to impale within the forest, or park of reasonable and conscionable gain, men who cared not how much they could extort out of poor men's hands for the loan of their money lent, and not to authorize any man to commit usury, as though it were lawful because it is permitted.

Therefore, those that say the laws there do allow of usury and license men to commit it freely do slander the laws and are worthy of reprehension. For although the laws say, Thou shalt not take above 2 shillings in the pound, 10 pound in a hundred, and so forth, doth this prove that it is lawful to take so much, or rather that thou shalt not take more than that? If I say to a man, Thou shalt not give him above one or two blows, doth this prove that I license him to give him one or two blows, or rather that he shall not give him any at all, or if he do, he shall not exceed or pass the bands of reasonable measure; so this law doth but mitigate the penalty? For it saith that the party that taketh but 10 pound for the use of an hundred pounds loseth but the 10 pounds, not his principal.

Spud. Then I perceive, if usury be not lawful by the laws of the realm, then is it not lawful by the laws of God.

Philo. You may be sure of that. For our Saviour Christ willeth us to be so far from covetousness and usury, as he saith: "Give to him that asketh thee, and from him that would borrow, turn not thy face away" (Matt. 5.6). Again, "Lend of thy goods to them who are not able to pay thee again, and thy reward shall be great in heaven" (Luke 6). If we must lend our goods then to them who are not able to pay us again, no not so much as the bare thing lent, where is the interest, the usury, the gain and overplus which we fish for so much? Therefore, our Saviour Christ saith, "It is more blessed to give than to receive." In 22 of Exodus, Deut. 23, Lev. 25, Neh. 5, Ez. 18 and many other places we are forbidden to use any kind of usury or interest, or to receive again any overplus besides the principal, either in money, corn, wine, oil, beasts, cattle, meat, drink, cloth, or anything else whatsoever. . . . In the 25 of Deut. the Lord willeth us not to crave again the thing we have lent to our neighbor. . . . If it be not lawful (then) to ask again that which is lent (for it is not the law of good conscience for them to exact it, if thou be abler to bear it, than the other to pay it), much less is it lawful to demand any usury or overplus. And for this cause the Lord saith, "Let there be no beggar amongst you, nor poor person amongst the tribes of Israel." Thus you see the word of God abandoneth usury even to hell, and all writers both divine and profane, yea, the very heathen people, moved only by the instinct of nature and the rules of reason, have always abhorred it. . . .

The usurer killeth not one but many, both husband, wife, children, servants, family, and all, not sparing any. And if the poor man have not wherewith to pay as well the interest as the principal, whensoever this greedy cormorant doth demand it, then suit shall be commenced against him. Out go butterflies and writs, as thick as hail, so the poor man is apprehended and brought *coram nobis* ["the error before us"—a legal procedure that protects defendants against arbitrary judicial action], and being once covenanted [i.e., bound over], judgment condemnatory and definitive sentence proceedth against him, compelling him to pay as well the usury and the loan of the money as the money lent. But if he have not to satisfy as well the one as the other, then to *Bocardo* [i.e., jail] goeth he as round as a ball, where he shall be sure to lie until he rot one piece from another without [i.e., unless] satisfaction be made. . . . Is this love? Is this charity? Is this to do to others as thou wouldest wish others to do to thee? . . .

We ought not to handle our brethren in such sort for any wordly matter whatsoever. We ought to show mercy and not cruelty to our brethren, to remit trespasses and offences rather than to exact punishment, referring all revenge to Him, who saith: *Mihi vindictam, et ego retribuam*: "Vengeance is mine, I will reward," saith the Lord.

Believe me, it grieveth me to hear (walking the streets) the pitiful cries and miserable complaints of poor prisoners in durance for debt, and like to continue there all their life, destitute of liberty, meat, drink (though of the meaner sort), and clothing to their backs, lying in filthy straw and loathsome dung, worse than any dog, void of all charitable consolation and brotherly comfort in this world, wishing and thirsting after death to set them at liberty and loose them from the shackles, gyves, and iron bands. Notwithstanding, some merciless tigers are grown to such barbarous cruelty that they blush not to say, truth, "He shall either pay me whole, or else lie there till his heels rot from his buttocks; and before I will release him, I will make dice of his bones." But take heed, thou devil (for I dare not call thee a man), lest the Lord say to thee as he said to that wicked servant (who, having great sums forgiven him, would not forgive his brother his small debt; but catching him by the throat, said: "Pay that thou owest"): "Bind him hands and feet and cast him into utter darkness, where shall be weeping and gnashing of teeth."

QUESTIONS FOR WRITTEN AND ORAL DISCUSSION

1. Why did the church oppose usury? Are the bases in Scripture consistent? If not, what inconsistencies do you find that provided for the later acceptance of at least moderate interest on loans made to and by Christians? Explain the importance of translation of the biblical texts in this regard.

2. How did Protestants deal with the problem of usury? Were they all of one mind, or was there conflict among them, and if so, on what grounds? What was Calvin's view? How does *The Merchant of Venice* reflect the issues that Shakespeare and his contemporaries faced?

3. What was the Jewish view of usury? On what basis were Jews commanded by Scripture to lend money without interest to fellow Jews? Why were they permitted to take interest from non-Jews? Why did Rabbi Yehiel Nissim da Pisa warn against lending to Gentiles at interest? What did he recommend that Jews should do?

4. Shakespeare was not only a poet and playwright, he was also a businessman. Examine a standard biography and see what kinds of commercial enterprises he and/or his colleagues in the theater engaged in. Did they give or take any loans at interest?

5. Discuss the Act against Usury that the English Parliament passed in 1571. If the act was designed to repress usury, how can one account for the limit of 10 percent permitted on loans? On what basis was it permitted? Did actual practice influence the act? What were the strongest arguments used for and against the act?

6. Compare the arguments of the Preacher and the Lawyer in Wilson's *Discourse upon Usury*. Which are the most compelling arguments on either side? Which ones probably influenced Parliament in 1571? Compare Shylock's justification of his "usances" in *The Merchant of Venice* with the Lawyer's arguments.

7. Antonio in *The Merchant of Venice* says that he neither borrows nor lends upon interest (1.3.66–67). Why is he willing to make an exception to help Bassanio? How does Shylock justify lending at interest? Is his reference to Scripture, that is, his story of Jacob and Laban (1.3.68–87), appropriate? On what basis does Antonio reject it?

8. By the end of 1.3 Shylock is willing to lend Antonio the 3,000 ducats he requests at no interest. Why is this unusual—in fact, an extraordinary gesture—for Shylock? What does he hope to gain by it? Would the bond and its forfeit stand up in a court of law today?

9. Discuss the dialogue between Spudeus and his friend Philoponus in Stubbes's *Anatomy of Abuses*. What does Philoponus say about the

practice of lending interest in Ailgna? Does he accurately reflect the practice in the England of his time? What is the point of Spudeus's questions? Is he presenting a counterargument, or leading Philoponus to register stronger arguments against usury? Analyze the rhetorical tactics Stubbes uses here.

10. Note the vivid description Philoponus gives of debtors held in prison in Ailgna. To what extent is this an accurate representation of actual practice in sixteenth-century England? You may wish to compare later treatments of the problem, for example, in novels such as *Bleak House* by the nineteenth-century English author, Charles Dickens.

SUGGESTED READING AND WORKS CITED

Baker, J. Wayne. "Heinrich Bullinger and the Idea of Usury." *Sixteenth Century Journal* 5 (1974): 49–70.

Cohen, Walter. "*The Merchant of Venice* and the Possibilities of Historical Criticism." *ELH* 49 (1982): 765–89.

Greaves, Richard L. *Society and Religion in Elizabethan England*. Minneapolis: University of Minnesota Press, 1981.

Jones, Norman. *God and the Moneylenders: Usury and Law in Early Modern England*. Oxford: Blackwell, 1989.

Robinson, Jack Hughes. *John Calvin and the Jews*. New York: Peter Lang, 1992.

Wilson, Thomas. *A Discourse upon Usury*. 1572. Edited by R. H. Tawney. New York: Harcourt Brace and Co., n.d.

7

Contemporary Applications and Interpretation

The issues raised in Shakespeare's *The Merchant of Venice* are of perennial interest. Not only the problems of anti-Semitism and racism, but those relating to the position of women in society, the quest for a mate, male friendships, and the rise of capitalism continue to preoccupy us today. Though a good deal of progress has been made in at least ameliorating some of the problems, many are far from being solved in a fully satisfactory way.

ANTI-SEMITISM AND RACISM

Despite the enormity of the Holocaust, in which six million Jews perished in Europe under the Nazis, anti-Semitism continues today. Some groups deny that the holocaust actually happened. Others uphold Adolf Hitler as a hero, preach his racist propaganda of the master race, and follow his example by engaging in violence and terrorism against Jews and other minorities, such as blacks in America and elsewhere, and Turks in Germany. Jewish cemeteries are desecrated, synagogues bombed or defaced, children attacked and shot in day-care centers. Organizations such as the so-called World Church of the Creator strongly advocate white supremacy.

Some of their members have gone on shooting rampages against imagined enemies, usually Jews or other minority groups.

Many intellectuals have pondered the phenomenon of anti-Semitsim and written countless books and articles on the subject, trying to understand what underlies the thinking of those who spouse racial or religious prejudice. Shortly after World War II, even before the full extent of the Holocaust was known, the French existentialist philosopher Jean-Paul Sartre explored the issue in *Anti-Semite and Jew* (1948). The roots of anti-Semitism, he believed, lay in the anti-Semite's feelings of mediocrity. Anti-Semitism, he wrote, "is an attempt to give value to mediocrity as such, to create an elite of the ordinary." Since, to the anti-Semite, intelligence is Jewish, it must be opposed, along with all other virtues that Jews possess. The anti-Semite chooses mediocrity out of fear of being alone and attempts to establish a new aristocracy—an aristocracy of mediocrity—so that he or she may claim superiority over others, particularly over Jews. Sartre sums up his views in the following paragraph:

[The anti-Semite] is a man who is afraid. Not of the Jews, to be sure, but of himself, of his own consciousness, of his liberty, of his instinct, of his responsibilities, of solitariness, of change, of society, and of the world—of everything except the Jews. He is a coward who does not want to admit his cowardice to himself; a murderer who represses and censures his tendency to murder without being able to hold it back, yet who dares to kill only in effigy or protected by the anonymity of the mob. . . . In espousing antisemitism, he does not simply adopt an opinion, he chooses himself as a person. He chooses the permanence and impenetrability of stone. . . . The Jew only serves him as a pretext; elsewhere his counterpart will make use of the Negro or the man of yellow skin. The existence of the Jew merely permits the antisemite to stifle his anxieties at their inception by persuading himself that his place in the world has been marked out in advance, that it awaits him, and that tradition gives him the right to occupy it. Antisemitism, in short, is fear of the human condition. The antisemite is a man who wishes to be pitiless stone, a furious torrent, a devastating thunderbolt—anything except a man.

While Antonio's anti-Semitism may not entirely fit Sartre's analysis in every respect, in some respects it does, especially the comments in the first and last sentences, which may provide a clue to

what underlies his enigmatic first line in *The Merchant of Venice*:
"In sooth, I know not why I am so sad." Possibly it is his fear of
his own consciousness, as Sartre says, of his liberty, responsibilities, instincts, and—the friends who surround him notwithstanding—his solitariness. For at the end of the play, as at the beginning,
Antonio is a lonely person. He may also be afraid of the changes
taking place in society and the world, as represented in Shylock's
profession as usurer and the beginnings of investment capitalism
that he personifies. Whatever the case, the anti-Semite, as Sartre
shows, is a pitiful individual, hardly a hero; someone desperately
trying to assert his or her superiority over others, as in a way Antonio does by forcing Shylock to renourice Judaism and convert to
Christianity at the end of the trial scene.

While Jews are often and typically the target of hate groups, they
are not the only ones, as Sartre recognizes. In recent times gay
men and women have also become targets. The following extract
from an article written by Tom Tugend for the Jewish Telegraphic
Agency in July 1999, gives a good, brief account of the activities of
one of the most notorious hate groups operating in the United
states today.

FROM TOM TUGEND, "SYNAGOGUE ARSON SUSPECTS KEPT
'HIT-LIST' OF SACRAMENTO-AREA JEWS"
(Jewish Telegraphic Agency, July 12, 1999)

LOS ANGELES, July 12—
Two men linked to last month's arson attacks on three Sacramento
synagogues kept a possible "hit list" of 32 Sacramento-area residents,
most of them Jewish, an investigator said.

The list was found during a search of the home of two brothers arrested as suspects in the killing of a gay couple.

The list includes officials of the Sacramento synagogues and congregation members who were quoted in the media after the attacks.

Those listed were briefed Friday by James Maddock, the FBI special
agent in charge of the arson investigation. They were told not to divulge
their names to the media and were promised added security.

In addition to the murders and arsons, the men may have connections
to the white supremacist World Church of the Creator, a member of
whom went on a shooting rampage in the Midwest during the July 4
weekend, killing two people and wounding six others.

According to reports in the Sacramento Bee and the Los Angeles Times,

Maddock said during the briefing that "we are virtually certain" that the two arrested brothers are connected with the arson attacks.

The brothers, Benjamin Matthew Williams, 31, and James Tyler Williams, 29, were apprehended last week in connection with the shooting deaths of Gary Matson, 50, and Winfield Mowder, 40.

The victims, who were longtime companions, and the Williams brothers lived near Redding, a town in rural northern California.

The names of several prominent Redding Jews were included on the "hit list" and law enforcement officials have advised the town's only synagogue, Temple Beth Israel, to beef up security.

Murder charges against the Williams brothers are expected to be filed shortly, investigators said. At this point, they have been charged with possession of stolen property, based on a purchase they made with the credit card belonging to one of the slain men. They are being held in jail on $150,000 bail each.

Neighbors described former high school honor students Matthew and Tyler Williams, who go by their middle names, as fervently religious "Bible-thumpers."

During the search of the brothers' home, investigators found a torn piece of paper that matched the tear on a piece discovered after the Sacramento arson at Congregation B'nai Israel, one of the three targeted synagogues.

Also discovered at the home were a large cache of semi-automatic weapons and hate literature, including pamphlets from the World Church of the Creator.

The Illinois-based racist group, which has several chapters in northern California, has been under close scrutiny since the arson attacks, during which the prepetrators left fliers blaming the "International Jew World Order" and the "International Jewsmedia" for the war in Kosovo.

The scrutiny has intensified since the shooting rampage [at a Los Angeles day-care center] by Benjamin Nathaniel Smith, a former member of the white supremacist group.

The FBI's Maddock said in Sacramento that the California investigations are being coordinated with other federal agents across the country. The probe may extend to a possible "widespread hate-crime conspiracy," the Sacramento Bee reported.

In an extensive report, the Anti-Defamation League has described the World Church of the Creator as one of the country's fastest-growing and most dangerous hate groups. ADL officials have petitioned U.S. Attorney General Janet Reno for a full field investigation of the church.

Meanwhile in Sacramento, moral and financial help continues to arrive from across the country to the three arson-struck synagogues, Congregation B'nai Israel, Congregation Beth Shalom, both Reform, and the Orthodox Knesset Israel Torah Center.

For decades the Anti-Defamation League has been in the fore-front combating religious and racial prejudice of all kinds, not only anti-Semitism. Liberal-minded Jews were in the vanguard of the American civil rights movement from almost the very beginning, and some even gave their lives while working alongside African Americans in the South. It is both paradoxical and sad, therefore, to find black anti-Semitism developing in the United States in recent years, fostered by people such as Louis Farrakan. Part of this anti-Semitism derives from resentment in the past among African Americans against Jewish shopkeepers and landlords, to whom (like Antonio in *The Merchant of Venice*) they owed money for rent or installment debts. The "pound of flesh" has become a cliché for any kind of interest payment that is regarded, rightly or wrongly, as exorbitant.

Portia's comments about her suitors (1.2), as well as her remark about the Prince of Morocco (2.7.79), reflect both racial prejudice and a form of nationalist pride that approaches xenophobia. While she does not use the derogatory nicknames for those of other nationalities or races that unfortunately riddle common parlance today, she reveals her feelings of superiority. In the context of the play, that signifies an ascendancy over anyone who is not an Italian aristocrat, like herself or Bassanio. In our time and in our country, a kind of inverted racism has developed, although it is not truly inverted at all—it is just another form of racial prejudice. The *New York Times* columnist, Bob Herbert, who is African American, often writes about contemporary racism, as in the following op-ed essay published in the *Times* concerning the racism among African Americans directed against whites and especially against Jews.

FROM BOB HERBERT, "ENDLESS POISON"
(*New York Times*, August 29, 1999)

In October 1985 Louis Farrakan brought his message of hate to Madison Square Garden, where he spent a couple of hours ranting about white people in general and Jews in particular before an audience of 25,000. It was a nauseating performance, filled with taunts and threats and pathetic extremes of self-absorption.

"I seem to have become quite a controversial fellow," Mr. Farrakan would say smiling. "Everywhere Farrakan goes, there's controversy around this fellow. There has not been a black man in the history of America that has been as repudiated as Brother Farrakan." And so on. . . .

Thousands cheered. It was very weird.

Among his many ugly outbursts that night was the question Mr. Farrakan raised about whether black leaders who opposed him should be allowed to live. He mentioned David Dinkins by name. Mr. Dinkins was the City Clerk [of New York; later the mayor] and had issued a public statement that said: "In light of Minister Farrakan's visit to New York, I must say that I find his blatantly anti-Semitic remarks offensive, and I condemn them."

Mr. Farrakan wondered if the death penalty might not be appropriate for such an offense. He told the crowd:

"The reason David Dinkins would do that is because they [black leaders] don't fear us. They fear white people. What I'm suggesting to black people is that the leaders have to begin to fear the people they say they represent. Because when the leader sells out the people, he should pay a price for that. Don't you think so? Do you think the leader should sell out and then live? . . ."

Now, nearly a decade and a half later, comes Khalid Abdul Muhammad with his act—a low-budget, street-corner version of the Farrakan road show. Mr. Muhammad despises—you guessed it—white people in general and Jews in particular, and his supporters recently took it upon themselves to punish a black leader who had the temerity to object to their rot.

Councilman Bill Perkins, a consistent critic of Mr. Muhhamad's so-called Million Youth March, was surrounded and harassed by a group of Mr. Muhammad's followers on Monday night. Mr. Perkins said they were pulling on his arm and yelling: "We are going to kill Uncle Toms like you. You are supposed to be supporting us."

Are we tired of this yet? Have we had our fill? The reason this sort of thing continues to erupt in places like Harlem is that so many black leaders have refused for so long to unequivocally oppose the racists, the anti-Semites, and the perpetrators of violence within the black community.

Almost always there were denunications and rationalizations. Denunciations of anti-Semitic outbursts by Mr. Farrakan and Mr. Muhammad, for example, were frequently accompanied by expressions of support for the "positive" aspects of their message.

There is no positive aspect. Those who think a hateful approach might somehow be good for children should check with Mr. Perkins's 10-year-old nephew, Klare, who is being raised by the Councilman. "He was frightened by what he saw on TV," said Mr. Perkins, "and expressed some concern about whether they knew where we lived."

In New York last week there was some evidence that this misguided tolerance might be eroding. After the attack on Mr. Perkins, several elected black officials stepped forward to denounce Mr. Muhammad, his message, and his march. Charles Rangel, the Congressman, said: "We hoped last year if there was an increase in kids coming, the good would overcome the hatred of the organizers. But after the events of last year, we could not encourage anyone to get involved in the event." Assemblyman Keith L. T. Wright declared "Enough is enough."

This should never have been a tough call. I don't remember too many black people looking for the constructive side of George Wallace or David Duke [i.e., two white supremacists].

Given our tragic history, the purveyors of hatred and violence should be pariahs in the black community as nowhere else. We're making some progress. Mr. Muhammad is having a more difficult time than he ever expected. But we're not there yet.

Progress is being made elsewhere as well. In a recent visit to Moscow, Abraham Foxman, the director of the Anti-Defamation League, compared the Moscow of 1999 with that of 1974, when he first visited the city, then under Soviet rule. The government no longer sponsors anti-Semitism, and Jews are free to emigrate and practice their religion openly. Yet anti-Semitism persists. The Communist parliamentarian, Albert Makashov, continues to make incendiary anti-Semitic statements, and in the spring of 1999 the director of Moscow's Jewish Cultural Center was critically stabbed in the chest by a young man who invaded his synagogue office and whose shirt concealed a large black swastika drawn in ink on his chest.

On the more positive side, and to the surprise of many, the internationally famous conductor, Zubin Mehta, led an orchestra consisting of 170 musicians from the Bavarian State Orchestra and the Israeli Philharmonic in a concert near the site of the infamous concentration camp of Buchenwald. It was the first time that the Israeli Philharmonic had performed on German soil in what was an emotionally charged atmosphere. It showed, according to some, that events of the past could be overcome, as the musicians sat together to play Gustav Mahler's Resurrection symphony. It also gave hope, according to Daniel Barenboim, another distinguished maestro, who has been working with young Israeli and Arab musicians, that reconciliation may be possible between those groups as well.

Finally, it is worth quoting in full the letter that John Cardinal O'Connor, Archbishop of New York, wrote to many Jewish leaders such as Elie Wiesel on September 8, 1999, on the eve of the Jewish High Holy Days.

FROM A LETTER BY JOHN CARDINAL O'CONNOR, ARCHBISHOP OF NEW YORK
(*New York Times* September 19, 1999)

My Dearest Friends:

The Jewish High Holy Days come once again, reminding our world of who created it, who blesses it with life and who judges it in his merciful justice. G-d, who gives all humanity the dignity of being made in his image, has chosen Israel as his particular people that they may be an example of faithfulness for all the nations of the earth. With sincere love and true admiration for your fidelity to the Covenant, I am happy once again to send my greetings for a blessed New Year.

This Sabbath evening, as the celebration of Rosh Hashanah commences, a new decade will begin. During the year of 5760 [in the Jewish calendar] we Christians will start a new era of the year 2000, the turn of another millennium in our history. Our Holy Father, Pope John Paul II, has asked all Christians to enter this new millennium in the spirit of Jubilee. Part of the process of Jubilee is a call for *teshuva*, or repentance. Ash Wednesday, March 8th, has been specially set aside as a day for Catholics to reflect upon the pain inflicted on the Jewish people by many of our members over the last millennium. We most sincerely want to start a new era.

I pray that as you begin a new decade, and as we begin another millennium in our Jewish-Christian relationship, we will refresh our encounter with a new respect and even love for one another as children of G-d. Working in our own ways, but also working together, let us both remain committed to the fulfillment of G-d's reign. I ask this Yom Kippur that you understand my own abject sorrow for any members of the Catholic Church, high or low, including myself, who may have harmed you or your forebears in any way.

Be assured of my prayers and friendship. L'shanah tovah tikotevu! [Happy New Year!]

> Faithfully,
> John Cardinal O'Connor
> Archbishop of New York
> (September 8, 1999)

QUESTIONS FOR WRITTEN AND ORAL DISCUSSION

1. Analyze Sartre's views on the causes of anti-Semitism. Are these the main causes, or the only ones? Has he omitted other possible causes, such as jealousy and envy of Jewish successes?

2. "The Protocols of the Elders of Zion" is an infamous piece of anti-Semitic propaganda, a document forged in Russia at the beginning of the twentieth century that purports to prove an international conspiracy of Jews to attain world power and overthrow Christianity. It has been frequently translated and circulated among many countries. What motivates such documents, and what makes people give them credibility? Are you aware of similar anti-Semitic propaganda or racist materials, and if so, what are they and where do they originate?

3. Many Christians believe that Jews should convert to their religion. In September 1999, for example, Southern Baptists in the United States urged church members to pray for Jewish conversions when the High Holy Days of Rosh Hashanah and Yom Kippur occurred during that month. Some Jewish leaders, although arguing that Baptists have a right to believe what they believe, found this offensive. Proselytizing is against Jewish practice and Jews do not attempt to convert others to Judaism. Compare the Baptists' motives and those of "Jews for Jesus" and similar groups with Antonio's demand that Shylock convert.

4. Given traditional support of Jews for the civil rights of all people and Jewish activism during the civil rights movement in the 1950s and 1960s, what do you think underlies black anti-Semitism? Why have some African-American leaders been slow to oppose men like Louis Farrakan and Khalid Abdul Muhammad?

5. Holocaust observances and Holocaust studies have become widespread in America. What are their aims? What are the aims of those who claim that the Holocaust never happened?

6. Write an essay on the work of the Anti-Defamation League and its efforts to combat worldwide anti-Semitism and other forms of religious and racial intolerance. To what extent have these efforts been successful? Are you aware of similar efforts in your community?

7. Besides the efforts of Zubin Mehta and Daniel Barenboim, what other attempts have been made throughout the world toward reconciling age-old prejudice and intolerance? Have they been successful? What efforts at the local level, at your school, for example, need to be made, and how should they be implemented?

8. Analyze carefully Cardinal O'Connor's letter to his friends on the eve of the Jewish High Holy Days. To what injuries against Jews does he

refer? Why do you think the Pope set aside Ash Wednesday (8 March 2000) as a day of repentance especially for the pain inflicted on Jews over the centuries? What kinds of cooperation do he and Cardinal O'Connor look forward to between Catholics and Jews? Should other sects follow their exhortation, and if so, how?

SUGGESTED READINGS

Allport, Gordon W. *The Nature of Prejudice*. Cambridge, MA: Addison-Wesley, 1954.

Calisch, E. N. *The Jew in English Literature*. 1909 Reprint, Port Washington, NY: Kennikat Press, 1969.

Dershowitz, Alan M. *Chutzpah*. Boston: Little, Brown, 1991.

Glock, Charles Y., and Rodney Stark. *Christian Beliefs and Anti-Semitism*. New York: Harper and Row, 1966.

Gross, John. *Shylock: Four Hundred Years in the Life of a Legend*. London: Chatto and Windus, 1992.

Lewis, Bernard. *Semites and Anti-Semites: An Inquiry into Conflict and Prejudice*. New York: Norton, 1986.

WOMEN, MARRIAGE, AND THE FAMILY

"You've come a long way, baby," or so, speaking of women, a television advertisement used to declare. Indeed, women have come a long way, if we compare their rights and privileges today with those they had—or rather, did not have—as recently as the 1920s, when women in America finally won the right to vote. Women still must battle against the "glass ceilings" and "sticky floors" in many businesses which, despite laws against sex discrimination, have a very tiny percentage of female executives at the highest levels. So, when a woman, Fiorina Carleton, was recently appointed head of the Hewlett-Packard Corporation, the move was declared a landmark in the advancement of women in business.

While Portia may have obtained her knowledge of Venetian law from her relative in Padua, Dr. Bellario (3.4.47–55), or at least as much as she needs to help Antonio, as a woman she could not have attended any of Italy's universities to study law. Today, in America, law schools freely admit qualified women, and prestigious law firms hire them. By 1990 women made up 40 percent of law school enrollments, and 20 percent of practicing lawyers were women, as compared with 4 percent women enrollments and 3 percent practicing lawyers a decade earlier. The numbers have grown since. Nevertheless, in many fields of activity, women still have to struggle against discrimination and, worse, sexual harassment. Patriarchy, moreover, is far from dead, not only in countries across Asia, Africa, and the Middle East, but also in the United States.

Patriarchy, as the British scholar Sylvia Walby defines it in *Theorizing Patriarchy* (1990), comes under two headings, private and public patriarchy:

In private patriarchy it is a man in his position as husband or father who is the direct oppressor and beneficiary, individually and directly, of the subordination of women. This does not mean that household production is the sole patriarchal structure. Indeed it is importantly maintained by the active exclusion of women from public arenas by other structures. The exclusion of women from these

152 Understanding *The Merchant of Venice*

other spheres could not be perpetuated without patriarchal activity at these levels.

Public patriarchy is a form in which women have access to both public and private arenas. They are not barred from the public arenas, but are nonetheless subordinated within them. The expropriation of women is performed more collectively than by individual patriarchs. The household may remain a site of patriarchal oppression, but it is no longer the main place where women are present. (p. 178)

Patriarchy as an issue, and as *The Merchant of Venice* depicts some aspects of it, has been publicized in America by the advent of an organization and movement called the Promise Keepers. Intended as an effort to restore and reinvigorate the nuclear family as an integrated unit, not only among African Americans but among all people, the movement has been opposed by feminist organizations who see it as an attempt to reverse the gains made in recent decades in obtaining equity with men. On its web page, for example, the National Organization for Women (NOW) has published a number of quoted remarks, such as those by Tony Evans, a prominent spokesperson that they claim show the real purpose of the Promise Keepers.

The demise of our community and culture is the fault of sissified men who have been overly influenced by women. (Tony Evans)

Don't you understand, mister, you are royalty and God has chosen you to be priest of your home? (Tony Evans)

It appears that America's anti-Biblical feminist movement is at last dying, thank God, and is possibly being replaced by a Christ-centered men's movement. (Rev. Jerry Falwell)

To the Promise Keepers's claim that the movement is good for women, NOW responds: "As feminists, we have long urged men to take responsibility in the home, as the Promise Keepers claim to do. However, when they say 'taking responsibility' they mean **taking control**. Promise Keepers openly call for wives to 'submit' to the husbands." Feminists argue that the Promise Keepers do not encourage a relationship of equality in a marriage; they maintain that Promise Keepers argue that men should assert their role as the head, or in other words, reestablish patriarchy as it appears in the Bible. Posing as a religious movement, the organization, while supported by the religious right, is politically motivated and active.

While the Promise Keepers may be a fringe group in America, they do represent an attitude toward patriarchy that indicates how some men feel about the gains women have made and continue to make in challenging the male hierarchy. Women's rights were substantially assisted by the Civil Rights Act of 1964, which stated under Title VII that

> It shall be unlawful employment practice for an employer to fail or refuse to hire or discharge any individual, or otherwise to discriminate against any individual with respect to his compensations, terms, conditions, or privileges of employment, because of such individual's race, color, religion, sex, or national origin.

The Equal Employment Opportunity Commission (EEOC) was established under the Civil Rights Act of 1964 and charged with enforcement of Title VII. The regulations the commission devised sought, and in large part succeeded in getting, states to revise laws that in effect discriminated against females under the guise of protecting them from jobs for which they were regarded as incapable or unsuitable or which were deemed dangerous.

As a result of this legislation and the establishment of the EEOC, a number of lawsuits were brought by women who felt they had been unfairly discriminated against. One such case is *Sprogis v. United Air Lines, Inc.* (1971), as recorded in Winnie Hazou's chapter, "Women and Employment," in her book, *The Social and Legal Status of Women* (1990). Mary Burke Sprogis was discharged from her job as a flight attendant when she married, but as the airline had no policy restricting employment to single males, Sprogis claimed discrimination and won her case. Today many female flight attendants are married and continue to work competently at their jobs.

A couple of years later, Dolores M. Meadows brought a class-action suit against the Ford Motor Company when 935 workers were hired for the production line in a plant in Kentucky, but none of them were women, although fifty-four women had applied. The company's policy, which involved minimum weight requirements for the job, was found to be highly discriminatory, notwithstanding its apparently neutral rules, which did not explicitly exclude women.

In universities, a number of women faculty members have also won suits that alleged discrimination against promotion and tenure, with the result that today departments are far more careful not only to seem, but to be gender neutral in making appointments, promotions, and awarding tenure. Many hitherto all-male universities, such as Yale and Columbia, have since admitted women, as have many private clubs, such as the Friars Club of California.

In their book *Megatrends for Women* (1992), Patricia Aburdene and John Naisbitt survey some professions, such as law and medicine, that have successfully attracted more women. They state that women earn 40 percent of the law degrees and one-third of the medical degrees. Women now make up more than a quarter of the number of practicing physicians, according to the Bureau of Labor Statistics, and more than half the number of primary-care doctors, they report. These statistics may be somewhat out of date by now but will be worth checking to see if they have increased or fallen in the last decade.

Women doctors are proving themselves to be different from their male counterparts in a variety of ways, Aburdene and Naisbitt claim. They are more careful and attentive listeners, show greater empathy for their patients, and avoid authoritarian attitudes usually associated with doctors in the past. Moreover, they take a greater interest in women's medical problems. The American Medical Association states that more than 100,000 women are practicing physicians.

Although a supposed overabundance of physicians has been reported so that the position of "doctor" is not making many "hot-job" lists lately, the field continues to attract women. The reasons are several: salaries remain high, health care is still a growth area, and more specialties that interest women have emerged, such as adult women's medicine. Meanwhile, more and more women are demanding female physicians, especially as "the menopause megatrend" develops, say Aburdene and Naisbitt.

But the best paying job for women among the professions is in field of law: "Women attorneys are already bringing home the big bucks" (Aburdene and Naisbitt 1992, 79). Citing the Bureau of Labor Statistics for 1991, the authors conclude that lawyer is the best-paying job for women, and they further cite the projection that the demand for lawyers and judges will increase by 35 percent between 1990 and 2005. Again, it will be worth checking to see if this projection is being realized.

The "hot-jobs" list for 1991 included environmental attorney and bankruptcy lawyer, although there was a considerable discrepancy between the earnings in each field. "Bankruptcy lawyers earned more than any other job in the 1991 Working Women list" (Aburdene and Naisbitt 1992, 80), and the figure they mention is a *starting salary* of $60,000 to $90,000 a year, compared to $26,000 for environment lawyers starting out in a federal agency and $45,000 to $50,000 in a private law firm. It is still a lot of money, but it is clear where the "big bucks" are.

On the other hand, women do not appear to be making similar inroads in other fields, such as those for airline pilots, law-enforcement officers, sports reporters and broadcasters, where the percentages range from a low of 4 percent (airline pilots) to a high of 14 percent (law-enforcement officers). "The numbers may be daunting," Aburdene and Naisbitt say, "but each percentage represents change at the roots of society." They note the policewoman whose "life is on the line protecting a community," the sportswriter who must endure sexual harassment in men's locker rooms, and other female workers in traditionally male-dominated jobs who have to work hard to earn the respect of their male colleagues. Yet, they conclude, "each is challenging individual perceptions about women on a daily basis. And that strengthens all women" (p. 81).

QUESTIONS FOR WRITTEN AND ORAL DISCUSSION

1. What are the aspects of private or public patriarchy in *The Merchant of Venice*, if any, that have remained fairly constant over the centuries? Which ones are still prevalent today, if not in modern American society, then elsewhere in the world? Give specific examples.

2. Is Portia a feminist? What other strong women characters does Shakespeare portray in any of his other plays you have read? Compare Portia, for example, with Rosalind in *As You Like It*, Beatrice in *Much Ado about Nothing*, and Viola in *Twelfth Night*. What aspects of modern feminism do they represent?

3. Compare the unions of Portia and Bassanio, Nerissa and Graziano, and Jessica and Lorenzo. Which one(s) portend patriarchy, either private or public? Why?

4. How valid are the arguments of the National Organization for Women (NOW) against the motives and goals of the Promise Keepers? Organize a debate on one of the major issues that divide these two groups.

5. What do you believe the position of husbands should be in the family? What indications are there in *The Merchant of Venice* that Bassanio, Graziano, or Lorenzo may assume that position?

6. What should the role of wives be in the family? What indications are there that Portia, Nerissa, or Jessica may assume or remain in that role?

7. What is the optimum relationship between husbands and wives in the family? What clues are there in *The Merchant of Venice* to support your views?

8. According to Sylvin Walby, "Women have citizen rights which are formally the same as those of men, but they form only a tiny proportion of the elected representatives, and a tiny proportion of the political agenda is around women's concerns" (1990, 180). Is this true in the United States? How many women serve in the House of Representatives? in the Senate? in your state legislature? What women's issues are currently in the forefront of political debate?

9. Has Title VII of the Civil Rights Act of 1964 been an effective weapon against gender discrimination? What kinds of gender discrimination—male or female—have been abolished in your community? What kinds persist, as far as you can tell?

10. Have any recent lawsuits been brought against companies or institutions in your geographical area charging sex discrimination? If so, describe the basis of the lawsuit and its outcome in the courts.

11. Using information you gather from the Bureau of Labor Statistics in Washington, DC, update the statistics you found in the discussion involving *Megatrends for Women*. Are they different today from the statistics compiled a decade ago? If so, do they trend upward or downward? To what do you attribute the differences?

12. What other professions besides medicine and law are attracting women today? Why? Are more women entering engineering, for example, or architecture? Are they earning as much as their male counterparts? Again, consult the Bureau of Labor Statistics for help.

13. Is your family doctor male or female? Have you had occasion to be examined by both genders? Do you notice any significant differences,

such as Aburdene and Naisbitt indicate? Does gender make for those differences, or can you attribute them to other factors, such as personality, training, or familiarity with your situation?

SUGGESTED READINGS AND WORKS CITED

Aburdene, Patricia, and John Naisbitt. *Megatrends for Women*. New York: Villard Books, 1992.

Chesler, Phyllis. *Patriarchy: Notes of an Expert Witness*. Monroe, ME: Common Courage Press, 1994.

Cornell, Drucilla. *At the Heart of Freedom: Feminism, Sex, and Equality*. Princeton: Princeton University Press, 1998.

Hazou, Winnie. *The Social and Legal Status of Women: Global Perspective*. New York: Praeger, 1990.

Matteo, Sherri, ed. *American Women in the Nineties: Today's Critical Issues*. Boston: Northeastern University Press, 1993.

Walby, Sylvia. *Theorizing Patriarchy*. Oxford: Blackwell, 1990.

Weiss, Penny. *Conversations with Feminism: Political Theory and Practice*. Lanham, MD: Rowman and Littlefield, 1998.

MALE FRIENDSHIP AND MALE BONDING

The women's movement has engendered a considerable amount of anxiety among men in some quarters. The anxiety stems from fears that women are taking control of society, not merely the family, with the result that men are becoming emasculated. Consequently, a men's movement has arisen. Although it has not achieved the same momentum as the women's movement, it remains appealing for various groups of men. The poet Robert Bly, author of *Iron John* (1990), for example, began in the 1990s to organize groups of men to engage not only in male bonding, but also in formulating an ideal of manhood that is viable today without at the same time becoming a threat to women or to the women's movement.

In 1994, A. Engler Anderson wrote about the men's movement and tried to define some of its goals as he perceived them in the movement's various aspects.

FROM A. ENGLER ANDERSON, "MALE BONDING"
(*The Jewish Exponent* [Philadelphia], December 16, 1994)

Shawn Israel Zevit likes going into the woods every month to commune with God and nature. The second-year student at the Reconstructionist College in Wynecote [Pennsylvania] is an activist in the burgeoning Jewish men's movement.

Zevit, 35, tells of a ceremony in Carpenter's Woods in Mount Airy last winter. "You could see your breath in the air; you could see the stars and the moon. It was so clear. We were able to bear witness to the beauty around us, and we lined arms and scattered up this icy hill. Every time somebody slipped, there were two men on either side to hold that man up," Zevit says, citing the mutual support as an example of "what we have in our heritage and what we have to offer in the future."

. . . The Jewish men's movement, says Zevit, aims to provide a way for men to get together, relate and discuss mutual concerns. "We're finding ways for Jewish men and women to be together, but not in exclusivity, to discuss the impact of change," Zevit says, explaining that the Jewish men's groups are based on the same rationale as Jewish women's groups.

"We're looking for a safer place to discuss the impact of our feelings, and our hopes as men and women," he says. "Unlike the past, where separation was enforced, this becomes a supportive place by choice."

. . . Professor David Johnson, a mythology expert at the University of New Mexico, Albuquerque, attributes the rise of the general men's movement—often cited as the creation of Robert [Bly], author of *Iron John*—to the growing disillusionment of men. Johnson says the need for a men's movement, which largely centers on small support groups, stems from the changing role of men in this century, as well as from the women's movement.

Dominant themes are dealing with feelings of hurt, loneliness, and solitude as many men approach the disillusionment of middle age. Bly argues that men today all too often grow up without traditional male rites of passage and supporting male role models. Much of his philosophy revolves around the absence of the father in child-rearing.

The larger men's movement is often labeled "mytho-poetic" because of its emphasis on searching for a new male mythology to take the place of the male-dominant mythology that centers around domination, Johnson said. He and others believe the mytho-poetic movement has been distorted by media coverage and reduced to an image of urban men dressed as savages and banging on drums in the woods.

Zevit underscores that the Jewish men's movement is separate from the mytho-poetic movement. But the focus on reaching back to Jewish lore and dusting off Jewish rituals and making them relevant to Jewish men today seems not so far from what Bly supports.

QUESTIONS FOR WRITTEN AND ORAL DISCUSSION

1. In *The Merchant of Venice* what ideal of manhood is explicitly or implicitly indicated? Which of the various male characters most closely approximates it? From a study of some of Shakespeare's other plays, what appears to be Shakespeare's conception of the ideal man? See, for example, Hamlet's praise of his friend Horatio in *Hamlet* 3.2.53–73.

2. Is Antonio's melancholy a symptom that many modern men also experience? Why are none of his friends able to help him out of it? Does Engler's article on "Male Bonding" offer some clues?

3. In the light of Engler's essay, discuss the male friendships that Shakespeare depicts in *The Merchant of Venice*. Do they provide the kind of mutual support that Engler or Zevit see as valuable and helpful? If so, how; if not, why not?

4. What traditional male rites or rituals have modern men abandoned or lost? Which ones do you think should be revived? Do any appear in

The Merchant of Venice or in any other Shakespeare play you have read? Should they be revived?

5. In the preface to *Iron John*, Robert Bly says that today, by the time a man reaches the age of 35, he realizes that "the images of the right man, the tough man, the true man which he received in high school do not work in life." To what specific images do you think he refers, and why don't they work any more? Did they ever work? Do they work in *The Merchant of Venice* or in any other Shakespeare plays you have read or seen performed?

6. Mentoring is an important part of the men's movement. What kind of mentoring occurs in *The Merchant of Venice?* How effective is it? What kinds of mentoring are important to revive today?

7. Scholars have identified four significant obstacles to forming close male friendships: (1) male competitiveness, (2) the absence of role models from which to learn about friendships and handling intimate relationships, (3) homophobia, or the fear of overt demonstrations of tenderness and affections, (4) men's need to be in control of themselves and their situations. Are any of these obstacles apparent in *The Merchant of Venice?* in your own experience or the observed experience of others you known?

SUGGESTED READINGS

Bly, Robert. *Iron John: A Book about Men*. New York: Addison-Wesley, 1990.

Nardi, Peter. *Men's Friendships*. London: Sage, 1992.

Stein, Peter J. "Men and Their Friendships." In *Men in Families*, edited by Robert A. Lewis and Robert E. Salt. London: Sage, 1986.

Tiger, L. *Men in Groups*. New York: Random House, 1969.

USURY AND THE RISE OF CAPITALISM

Without question, the modern capitalist movement, which has its origins in the emergence and spread of banks in the Renaissance, owes a great deal of its success to the widespread use of lending money at interest—usury, as it is still called in some quarters. Although interest-free loans continue to be available for persons in need—through the Jewish Free Loan Society, for example—for most people, borrowing at interest is taken for granted. Interest is the charge a lender makes for the use of money or credit, usually figured as a percentage of the principal and computed either annually, quarterly, or monthly. Interest rates vary a great deal, not only from time to time, depending on the economy, but also on the amounts borrowed, the purposes for which loans are used, and the length of time required to repay them.

In America, more people own their own homes today than ever before, thanks largely to their ability to borrow money through mortgages. These loans require repayments usually on a monthly basis over a course of time ranging from ten to thirty years. Again, mortgage rates may vary according to market pressures, the time required for the loan, fixed or variable rates, and so forth. Many people today also borrow to buy automobiles, using two- to five-year loans with rates that vary accordingly. Moreover, in the last few decades, the use of credit cards has become widespread. While no interest is charged if payments are made within a given period (usually twenty-one days), a portion of the credit balance may be carried over from month to month at interest charged to the cardholder.

Big business chiefly uses loans from large money center banks to do their work, regardless of what it is—construction, import and export, manufacturing, etc. Shares of stock may be sold to help finance the operation of businesses, which may also depend in part on the sale of interest-bearing bonds. That interest derives from the profits earned by the company issuing the bonds. When the company is no longer profitable, it may default on the bonds, and both bondholders and shareholders may lose their investments. While large multinational corporations seldom fall into this predicament (often their national governments spring to their aid to prevent collapse, especially when thousands of jobs depend on keeping the corporation going and the overall economy on keel), small businesses may fail at a sometimes alarming rate. A case in point: when the Chrysler Corporation was in danger of going out of business some years ago, the United States government subsidized its financing through favorable loans until such time as the company recovered and once again became profitable. (It has since merged with the German automobile manufacturer, Daimler-Benz.)

Interest rates in the United States are controlled in two ways: by the federal government and by state laws and regulations. The federal government controls interest rates through the Federal Reserve Board, which sets the prime rate that the Federal Reserve Bank charges, and adjusts it from time to time, depending on the state of the economy. When the economy is heating up, the board tends to raise interest rates to slow economic growth, since businesses depend on the ability to borrow money to make a profit. When the economy is in danger of recession and needs a boost, the board may lower the prime rate. (The prime rate is the rate that banks charge their best customers; but many rates may exceed the prime rate by as much as two percentage points.) States have devised laws and regulations that permit interest rates to vary depending on the prime rate.

In the late 1970s and early 1980s, when inflation was rampant, interest rates soared in America, causing many states to adopt usury laws with strict penalties for charging interest above an allowed rate. California, for example, permits parties to contract for interest on a loan primarily for personal, family, or household purposes at a rate not exceeding 10 percent a year, based on the unpaid balance of the loan. For other loans, the allowable rate is 5 percent over the amount charged by the Federal Reserve Bank of San Francisco to member banks on the 25th day of the month before the loan. California usury laws, however, do not apply to real estate brokers if loans are secured by real estate. Limitations also do not apply to most lending institutions such as banks, credit unions, finance companies, pawnbrokers, and the like, although state laws place limitations on some of these loans but at a higher percentage rate than usury laws allow. Usury laws also do not apply to time payment contracts, such as retail installment contracts.

But allowable interest rates vary a good deal from state to state.

One state that has abandoned usury laws altogether is Delaware. As a result, many banks in the credit card business, such as Chase Manhattan Bank, Citibank, MBNA, and others, have set up shop in Delaware. That state is also very liberal in its corporation fees and corporate income taxes; hence, many companies have incorporated in Delaware, whose economy has become increasingly dependent on the income they bring to the state.

Many banks and finance companies require a good credit rating from a customer before a loan is approved; either that, or tangible security such as a house or other valuable possesion. For someone to offer a pound of flesh, however, is unheard of; moreover, no government would allow a citizen to offer his or her life as security for a loan, which is what Antonio does in *The Merchant of Venice*. Such a bond would be regarded as invalid in any civilized country. A good deal of case law exists to this effect. Citing Lawson's *Contracts*, E. J. White, the author of *Commentaries on the Law in Shakespeare*, says that "All contracts having for their object the taking of human life have always been regarded as void, because [they are] contrary to good morals." A more recent scholar, Daniel J. Kornstein, maintains that this doctrine (that contracts against the public good are void) is still very much alive today, and he refers to the laws of the state of New York and elsewhere to show that a usurious contract is unenforceable. Furthermore, insofar as Shylock made light of the bargain, by proposing the forfeit "in a merry sport" (1.3.142), an element of fraud tainted the negotiation. In our own time, Kornstein says, case reports are full of lenders who, violating usury laws, must, like Shylock, forfeit both principal and interest. But the so-called alien statute law that Portia invokes to further punish Shylock (4.1.43–58) is fundamentally flawed. It is not only extremely harsh, it also denies equal protection under the law. No comparable citizen statute exists, so far as we are told or Shylock is aware, to protect aliens against similar offenses by citizens. As such, the alien statute law, according to Kornstein, anticipates the infamous Nuremburg laws of Nazi Germany or the Jim Crow laws in America, fortunately long since abolished.

Although imagining a world without moneylending at interest may be inconceivable today, appeals for an end to usury have not ceased. As recently as April 14, 1999, according to the *Houston Catholic Worker*, Pope John Paul II called for an end to usury while addressing members of the National Council of Anti-Usury Foundations and their regional delegations. The same report notes that in 1997 Bishop Tarcisio Bertone, secretary of the Vatican Congregation for the Doctrine of the Faith, called for a new *encyclical* [i.e., papal letter] on the subject of usury and on the use of money in general. He referred specifically not only to the critical aspects of usury, but also to the issue of international loans that wind up creating more problems than they solve through the problem of international debt. Others, like the late poet Ezra Pound in his *Cantos* or writers for the *New Dawn* magazine in Australia, have also inveighed against usury. But it is important to recall the difference between usury, or exorbitant interest on money or goods lent, and reasonable interest, precisely as the Tudor politicians argued the case in 1571 (see Chapter 6).

QUESTIONS FOR WRITTEN AND ORAL DISCUSSION

1. What are the prevailing mortgage rates for homebuyers today? Are they usurious, in your opinion, or reasonable? What percentage of homeowners finance their homes with mortgages? Why does the Internal Revenue Service (IRS) allow deductions for interest payments on home mortgages?

2. What is a home equity loan? What are the prevailing interest rates on such loans? on personal loans? Do they seem excessive to you? Does the Internal Revenue Service also allow deductions for these loans? If so, why? What kinds of interest payments are not allowed by the IRS?

3. Did Antonio have to borrow money for the ships he sent abroad loaded with merchandise? If not, did he use cash only? Would such an enterprise be viable today on a cash-only basis?

4. At 1.1.180, Antonio sends Bassanio out to "Try what my credit can in Venice do." What does he mean? Why then does Bassanio go to Shylock? Why does Shylock at first hesitate when talking with Bassanio about the loan? What does he mean when he says Antonio is "sufficient"?

5. Would a bank or finance company lend money to Antonio today? If so, under what terms would it lend money to him? Would he be regarded as a good credit risk?

6. By act 3 Antonio is regarded as a bankrupt. What are the modern provisions for the protection of bankrupts today? Could Antonio stand in similar jeopardy to Shylock under contemporary bankruptcy laws?

7. Given the possible appeals to law (other than the alien statute law) that Portia might have used at the outset to declare Shylock's case against Antonio invalid, why does she pursue the process as she does? Is Shakespeare really interested in the legal arguments, or is he motivated in the trial scene by other concerns, such as the relationship of mercy to justice? Discuss.

8. Today, the International Monetary Fund (IMF) arranges for loans to underdeveloped countries. Write a research paper on the effectiveness of the IMF and its ability to help raise the standard of living in Third World countries. What are the usual terms of the loans?

SUGGESTED READINGS

Furlong, Carla. *Marketing Money*. Chicago: Probus Publishing, 1989.

Kaufman, Henry. *Interest Rates, the Markets, and the New Financial World*. New York: Times Books, 1986.

Kornstein, Daniel J. *Kill All the Lawyers? Shakespeare's Legal Appeal*. Princeton: Princeton University Press, 1994.

White, E. J. *Commentaries on the Law in Shakespeare*. 1913. Reprint, Littleton, CO: Fred B. Rothman, 1987.

THE MERCHANT OF VENICE IN PERFORMANCE

Next to *Hamlet, The Merchant of Venice* is Shakespeare's most frequently performed play. The reason for its apparent popularity may be in part because it is perennially a required text set for national examinations that students in British secondary schools take. It is less popular in the United States because of the anti-Semitism that the play incorporates, although many producers, directors, and actors have argued that while the play contains elements of anti-Semitism, it is not in itself anti-Semitic. Recently, some scholars have tried to show that, on the contrary, Shakespeare explores ways to reconcile the age-old antagonisms between Christians and Jews (see, for instance, Yaffe 1997).

The stage history of *The Merchant of Venice* is one of the most fascinating of all Shakespeare's plays. We have no evidence of the way Shylock was originally played. Very likely he was played as a comic villain, complete with red wig and red beard, in the manner of Marlowe's Barabas in *The Jew of Malta*. In the 1950s at the Oregon Shakespeare Festival, Angus Bowmer enacted the role in that manner, and to the surprise of many who had been brought up to view Shylock as a tragic hero, Bowmer's representation worked well. This is how Shylock was performed at the end of the seventeenth century and the beginning of the eighteenth century, if we may judge from the way Thomas Doggett enacted the role in George Granville's adaptation called *The Jew of Venice*. When Charles Macklin restored Shakespeare's text later in the eighteenth century, Shylock became a fierce villain, much in the way that Maria Edgeworth reconstructs his performance in her novel *Harrington* (1817).

In 1814, Macklin's interpretation gave way to Edmund Kean's more sympathetic portrayal of Shylock as a Jew "more sinned against than sinning." Kean's impassioned representation of Shylock as persecuted martyr reached its culmination in Henry Irving's production in 1879 which, like many nineteenth-century productions, heavily cut the text to accommodate elaborate scene shifts. But Irving also added a new scene in which Shylock returned home after the dinner at Bassanio's, only to find his daughter Jessica gone

Henry Irving as Shylock. Reproduced courtesy of
The Folger Shakespeare Library.

and his house empty. This interpolated scene has been revived in
some recent productions of the play that try to arouse as much
sympathy for Shylock as possible, as was done at performances at
the Shakespeare Theatre in Washington, DC, and the National Theatre in London, both in 1999.

The role of Portia, while less complex, has also attracted major
performers. Ellen Terry played opposite Henry Irving and was a
match for his Shylock. According to one critic, she was "all grace,
sparkle, piquancy, ardor, sweetness, and passion." But the role is
fraught with pitfalls: Portia has been played as too spirited and
flighty, as acted by Kitty Clive in Macklin's production, or too snob-
bish and sophisticated, as Joan Plowright enacted her in Jonathan
Miller's National Theatre production in 1970. Miller's production

was set in the Victorian period and starred Laurence Olivier as Shylock. His Shylock was a socially aspiring Jew, trying hard to emulate the magnificoes, like Antonio, who despised him only because of his religion. But after Jessica's elopement, he became an object more of pity than fear, lugubriously lamenting the loss of his daughter seemingly more than his ducats.

Jessica's last line in the play, "I am never merry when I hear sweet music" (5.1.69), has provided the subtext for some actors and directors who conceive of Jessica as one who has second thoughts about what she has done in abandoning her father, stealing his money and jewels, and eloping with Lorenzo. In Jonathan Miller's 1970 production, while the other couples merrily celebrate their reunions and reconciliations at the end of 5.1, she remains somber, drifting off by herself with the deed in her hand, as a cantor intones the Mourner's Kaddish from within (or voice-over in the television version). In Michael Kahn's production at the Shakespeare Theatre in Washington, Lorenzo turns out to be a gold-digging cad who treats Jessica roughly, thus giving her additional cause to feel dismay at what she has done, and in that production she too drifts off at the end holding Shylock's deed of gift in her hand.

The interpretation of Antonio has also varied a good deal from production to production. The enigma his character presents from his opening line to the end of the play allows actors to adopt different subtexts with which to approach his role. If his sadness stems from a latent or an overt homosexuality, he may be more or less demonstrative in his affection toward Bassanio. In some recent productions, such as one by the Royal Shakespeare Company in Stratford-upon-Avon in 1986, Antonio gave Bassanio a resounding kiss on the lips in the first scene and showed in later scenes how devoted he was to him. Other enactments of the role have played down this aspect of Antonio's character and showed him rather as a melancholy, middle-aged bachelor with no more than a fatherly interest in Bassanio, whom he supports financially. The play is filled with so many contradictions and inconsistencies involving so many characters that its rich ambiguity allows for many different interpretations and hence its continued fascination for playgoers.

In Shakespeare's time, historical authenticity in staging was held in little regard, and actors performed mainly in the dress of their own time with little scenery other than a painted backcloth. This tradition continued through the eighteenth century, although movable flats by then had been introduced to indicate scene changes. Not until the nineteenth century did actor-managers like Charles Kean take a serious interest in what has since been called archeological Shakespeare; that is, he and others made determined efforts to set the scene and the costumes accurately in the historical time period of the play.

In the twentieth century, some recent directors have revived the older notion of contemporary stage sets and costumes, and actors have performed in modern dress. A good example of a modern dress production was staged in 1991 in Sofia, Bulgaria, where Portia and Nerissa enter in 1.2 riding bicycles, and Belmont has a swimming pool. A better example was the Royal Shakespeare Company's production with David Calder as Shylock in 1993. The stage set for Shylock's office was a modern brokerage, complete with many computer screens. Lancelot Gobbo's first appearance brought the house down before he even uttered a word. Playing with one of the computer keyboards, he did something that suddenly made all the screens go blank. Christopher Luscomb, as Lancelot, wonderfully and comically showed his amazement and then tried to cover up the accident as well as he could, as the audience roared with laughter at his discomfiture.

The best insight this modern dress production afforded, however, was at the end of the trial scene. Unlike other productions that try to make Shylock a religious Jew, Calder's Shylock was a modern Jew whose religion was almost a secondary concern for him, as religion often is for many in this secular age. True, he wore a yarmulke, or skullcap, but unlike Laurence Olivier or Hal Holbrook (in Kahn's production) he did not swathe himself in a tallith, or prayer shawl, at any point. As a modern Jew rather than a Hassid (i.e., member of an orthodox sect), he was dressed accordingly, that is, in the business suit appropriate to an important man in the City of London, England's commercial center. Thus, at the end, when he is forced to convert to Christianity or lose the mercy of the duke, he does so with apparent ease. No offstage wail of anguish followed his departure from the scene, as it did Olivier's Shylock, for this Shylock was content indeed to have at least half his fortune left so he could continue in business. By setting the

play in this fashion, then, some of the sting of the forced conversion was removed, if not entirely.

FROM WILLIAM TRIPLETT, "THE SHYLOCK WITHIN"
(*The Washington Post*, May 30, 1999, pp. G1, 5)

Shylock the hated and hating Jew, [was] often played in Shakespeare's
time for ugly caricature. [Hal] Holbrook . . . sees a more complicated
character. He's not the first actor to sense that. . . . The first actor to portray Shylock with any kind of humanity was the great Edmund Kean, who
made his London debut in the role in 1814, astonishing audiences with
his passionate, fiery style. "To see Kean," Samuel Coleridge said, "is to
read Shakespeare by lightning." To some extent every actor since has
worked in Kean's shadow. Holbrook has studied the record of that sem-
inal performance, as well as those of many others who later attempted
the role. He's also heavily researched the history of Renaissance Jews.

Still at 74, his hair and beard a wild, silvery shock and grizzle, Holbrook
is of course best known for his stage impersonation of [Mark] Twain, to
which he brings a winning mix of wit, outrage and vulnerability. He's
also won five Emmy awards for roles in contemporary television dramas.

Yet Shakespeare is hardly a stranger to him. . . . About ten years ago he
started feeling it was time to come back to the boards and the Bard.
Acting for cameras had distracted him from assaying great roles such as
Richard III and Hamlet. If he wasn't careful, he might find himself too
old even to play Lear—which he finally did in 1990 at the Roundabout
Theatre in New York.

The next year he played Shylock—in a modern—setting production of
Merchant at San Diego's Old Globe Theatre. Despite some warm reviews
for his performance, Holbrook wasn't happy: He felt the updated setting
with its updated manners had blunted not just Shylock's character but
also the play's sharp antisemitism.

Several years afterward, he rang up Shakespeare Theatre Artistic Director Michael Kahn, whom he'd never met, and offered his services. Kahn
was intrigued: He'd heard good things about Holbrook's classical acting.
Plus, as Kahn puts it, "though I had done *Merchant* a long, long time
ago, my feeling was, 'Well, it's been long enough for me to have some
new ideas about it.' "

One idea was to use a modern setting. Holbrook immediately objected.
"I felt that this play can teach a more powerful lesson to us all about
intolerance and injustice if emotions are wide open and not restrained,"
the actor says. The play had to be done, he felt, in its original Renaissance

Hal Holbrook as Shylock in a production
by The Shakespeare Theatre, directed by
Michael Kahn (1999). Photo © Carol Rosegg.
Reproduced courtesy of The Shakespeare
Theatre.

era, when despising Jews, not to mention cutting a pound of flesh from
someone, was considered part of civilized society. Kahn agreed.

"The whole idea of injustice has always been a big, uh, emotional blur
in my life," Holbrook says. His resonant baritone goes flat. Suddenly he
doesn't seem quite comfortable.

It's 1927, Cleveland, and the 2-year-old Harold Holbrook learns his
mother has left the family. "We never knew why she left, but I'm sure
she had her reasons," he says matter-of-factly. "She was a very poor, very
young girl." A few days later his father disappears on a search for her.
Neither will ever return.

Young Holbrook goes to New England to live with relatives, who find
it perfectly acceptable to refer to Jews and other minorities by vulgar

names. "It embarrassed me," he says. When he was not being embarrassed, he was being beaten while attending an elite boys school. "I was
sent away to make a *man* of me," he says, disgust and anger evident in
his voice. The headmaster was "a little weirdo. We'd line up—they just
called your name out, and you went and lined up outside his office. One
by one you'd go in, be told to take your pants down—both of them—
grab the arms of an armchair and lean over. Then he took a packing crate
slat out of the closet and beat you until you cried."

That was the standard treatment. Holbrook, for some reason he's never
figured out ("there must have been something in my face"), drew special
attention. "At various times he slapped me, knocked me against the wall,
kicked me in the groin. I've never forgotten it." Relief finally came when
the headmaster, faced with mandatory retirement, took a gun and blew
his brains out. His suicide note, Holbrook remembers, said, "I can no
longer live without boys."

The worst part, Holbrook says, was never having been told why he was
being beaten. "You never knew what you did wrong. And you never knew
when it was coming." He pauses, then spits the word "sadist."

Emotional burr? Injustice—in particular, the abuse of power—is more
like a minor obsession with Holbrook. . . . He sees Shylock as a man to
whom similar injustice has been done. "When you read about the treatment of the Jews in the 14th, 15th, and 16th centuries . . . it's just *un-
believable*," he says, his voice now rising to the pitch of thunder. Add
the pain of his own boyhood to his research, and you have an idea of
the Shylock that Holbrook is portraying.

"The thing I love most about Shylock is he stood *up* for what he believed in. This is a man whose fury against the injustice practiced upon
him goes to the point of no restraint. When he starts to take that knife,
he knows he has broken the law of his religion, because it's *against* the
Jewish religion to shed blood like that. He is sinning, and he will *never*
be forgiven. . . . [T]his sweet little speech about 'the quality of mercy' is
pure hypocrisy as far as he's concerned! There *is* no mercy. There is only
retribution."

Implacably so.

QUESTIONS FOR WRITTEN AND ORAL DISCUSSION

1. Will Kempe, the most famous comedian of his day, and Richard Bur-
   bage, who performed leading roles, were both members of the Lord
   Chamberlain's Men when *The Merchant of Venice* was first performed.
   Imagine the ways each man would have performed Shylock, comically
   or tragically, comparing and contrasting their handling of several

scenes, especially 1.3. Describe their performances as you imagine them.

2. What makes *The Merchant of Venice* a popular play today? Do you see it as an effective treatment of intolerance and a means of combating religious and racial prejudice, or does it serve rather to reinforce prejudices that people may have? How much depends on the interpretation of the play on the stage?

3. How should Portia be portrayed? What indications are there that she is a spoiled little rich girl? Is she only that? What other aspects of her character does the play include, and how should they be enacted?

4. How justified do you think Michael Kahn was in directing Lorenzo to portray a cad who is only interested in getting Jessica for her money? Was this a misinterpretation of the role, or is his character sufficiently ambiguous in the text to allow for that interpretation?

5. In several recent productions, Lancelot Gobbo and his father are enacted by black actors, often with intended comic results. Are producers justified in casting black actors in the parts? Are they mainly using this as a means for providing additional roles for black actors in modern Shakespearean productions, or is it unintentionally demeaning? How do you think the roles should be cast and performed?

6. If the fifth act helps restore *The Merchant of Venice* more completely to the realm of comedy, should Jessica be played as having second thoughts about what she has done? Granted that interpretation adds a further dimension to the play, what further justification is there for it? Or is there any?

7. Other actors besides Hal Holbrook have given interviews or written articles about how they approach the role of Shylock. Using your library's research materials, find two or three accounts by other actors, such as the discussion by Patrick Stewart and David Suchet in John Barton's *Playing Shakespeare*. Compare and contrast their different interpretations, and argue for which representation you think is most convincing.

8. Compare Holbrook's views on modern-dress productions of *The Merchant of Venice* with reviews of productions like the Royal Shakespeare Company's in 1993, or the Old Globe's in which he himself performed. What do you see as the advantages or disadvantages of such productions? If you were staging the play, would you set it in the Renaissance or in your own time? Explain.

9. Jonathan Miller set his 1970 production of *The Merchant of Venice* in the Victorian period. That was a time when Jews were still discriminated against in England. (Baron de Rothschild, for example, was sev-

eral times elected to Parliament, but he was not allowed to take his seat until many years later.) Does this suggest a political agenda for the production? Should a political agenda influence an interpretation of this play? Any Shakespeare play? Give your reasons.

SUGGESTED READINGS AND WORKS CITED

Barton, John. *Playing Shakespeare*. London: Methuen, 1984.

Bulman, James. *Shakespeare in Performance: The Merchant of Venice*. Manchester: Manchester University Press, 1991.

Lelyveld, Toby. *Shylock on the Stage*. Cleveland: Press of Western Reserve University, 1960.

Odell, G.C.D. *Shakespeare from Betterton to Irving*. 2 vols. New York: Columbia University Press, 1920.

Overton, Bill. *Text and Performance: "The Merchant of Venice."* Atlantic Highlands, NJ: Humanities Press, 1987.

Yaffe, Martin D. *Shylock and the Jewish Question*. Baltimore: Johns Hopkins University Press, 1997.

Index

About the Author

JAY L. HALIO is Professor of English at the University of Delaware. He is author or editor of more than 20 books on Shakespeare and his contemporaries and also on modern American and British literature. His numerous publications on Shakespeare include *Romeo and Juliet: A Guide to the Play* (Greenwood, 1998), an edition of *The Merchant of Venice* for *The New Oxford Shakespeare*, and an edition of *King Lear* for *The New Cambridge Shakespeare*.